Praise for MoneyBags

"*MoneyBags* is full of practical, fun, and simple
tools to teach kids about money. Wendy presents
a complex and often taboo subject in a way that
empowers parents and kids alike."

—Deirdre Van Nest, PROFESSIONAL SPEAKER AND
PERFORMANCE COACH, WWW.FIREYOURFEAR.COM

"Some of the most powerful words in our language
are at the foundation of this wonderful, fun and
important new book by Wendy Gillespie. *MoneyBags*
is about prudence, choices, discipline, character, self-
reliance, family, and yes… it is also about money
and creating good money habits. Gillespie weaves
personal stories with philosophical principles. She
provides simple explanations for each concept
introduced, and she always provides an easy way to
get into action. What a gift we give, when we teach
our children, and grandchildren the truth
about money!"

—Ed Kelly, FOUNDER, SUMMIT JOURNEY COACHING

MONEYBAGS™

A Guide to Teaching your Kids About Money

Wendy Gillespie, MBA, CFP®

BEAVER'S
POND
PRESS

ISBN 13: 978-1-59298-947-8

Library of Congress Catalog Number: 2013922387

Printed in the United States of America

First Printing: 2014

18 17 16 15 14   5 4 3 2 1

Cover and interior design by James Monroe Design, LLC.

Beaver's Pond Press
7108 Ohms Lane
Edina, MN 55439–2129
952-829-8818

www.BeaversPondPress.com

To order, visit www.BeaversPondBooks.com or call 1-800-901-3480. Reseller discounts available.

Dedicated to my money mentors:
Louise (Mom), Phil (Dad), Imogene, and Ned (MoneyBags).

Thank you for taking the time
to teach me about money!

Contents

Foreword . . . . *xi*

Introduction *1*

PART 1: Getting Started

Chapter 1: Create Family Money Rituals 13

Chapter 2: Family Savings Jar 17

Chapter 3: Commit to Breaking the Cycle 21

Chapter 4: Money is a Permission Item 27

Chapter 5: Needs versus Wants 31

Chapter 6: Maslow's Hierarchy of Needs 33

Chapter 7: The Money Hierarchy 37

Chapter 8: The Importance of Discipline 47

Chapter 9: The Importance of
Giving an Allowance 53

Chapter 10: SAVE . . . Taxes . . . Share . . . Spend 59

Chapter 11: Taxes 67

Chapter 12: The Value of a Dollar:
Begin Using ONLY Cash 71

Chapter 13: You Need to Say NO 75

Chapter 14: Play Board Games That Focus
on Money. 79

PART 2: MoneyBags Mindset (Behavior and Skills)

Chapter 15: Money Personality Spectrum. 89

Chapter 16: The Myth that Rich People
are Mean and Evil. 95

Chapter 17: How Big is Their MoneyBag? 99

Chapter 18: All Actions Have Consequences 105

Chapter 19: Live within Your Means 109

Chapter 20: Budgeting 113

Chapter 21: Awareness of Ongoing Costs. 121

Chapter 22: Optimism 129

Chapter 23: Be Contrary 133

Chapter 24: The Power of Doubling. 137

Chapter 25: The Importance of
Delayed Gratification 141

Chapter 26: Layaway 147

Contents

Chapter 27: Out of Sight, Out of Mind 151

Chapter 28: The Thrill of the Hunt! 155

Chapter 29: Shopping With a Purpose. 161

Chapter 30: The Importance of Integrity 167

Chapter 31: Following the Rules 171

Chapter 32: Your Word is Law. 175

Chapter 33: Respectful and Responsible
to Things. 179

Chapter 34: Penny Wise and Pound Foolish 185

Chapter 35: Coupons!. 189

Chapter 36: Understanding Risk. 193

PART 3: MoneyBags Mechanics and Skills . . . How Money Works

Chapter 37: The Value of a Penny 199

Chapter 38: Counting Money 203

Chapter 39: Counting Money Back. 207

Chapter 40: Tipping 211

Chapter 41: The Importance of
Ballpark Numbers. 215

Chapter 42: The Importance of Having Your Kids
WORK for What They Want......... 219

Chapter 43: Profit.............................. 225

Chapter 44: Marketing is a
Double-Edged Sword 235

Chapter 45: The Impact of Stealing.............. 239

Chapter 46: Bartering.......................... 243

Chapter 47: Where Does Money Come From?...... 247

Chapter 48: What Happened to the Gold?........ 251

Chapter 49: Why Do People Use Banks?.......... 255

Chapter 50: Safety Deposit Box/Vault 259

Chapter 51: How Do Banks Make Money? 263

Chapter 52: Plastic Cards!....................... 267

Conclusion *275*

Acknowledgments........ *277*

About the Author *281*

Foreword

When I was a young boy growing up in North Dakota, I learned the value of a dollar by working at a bank and on a farm. At the bank where my dad was employed and a part owner, I was paid fifty cents a week to empty trash cans and tidy up. On the farm owned by my uncle and aunt I baled hay and I collected the fresh-laid eggs. I was paid two cents a bale for the hay and I collected the eggs without pay. Of course, I wasn't just learning the value of money, I was learning the value of work. I was beginning to develop good work habits, a sense of responsibility to work for my money and use it wisely once I made it.

Times have changed since then, but what has not changed is the significance we place on having money and the responsibility to work for it and use it wisely. Our relationship with money, how we make it and how we use it, is expressed through our behaviors and

MoneyBags

habits, directly influencing how we view, value, spend, and save money. I was taught to work for my money, save some, spend some, and give some away. I still do all of those things habitually and routinely.

Advances in neuroscience and psychology have found the link between repeated behaviors and habits to be true. Both behavior and habits are reinforced neuronal circuits within the brain that allow it to complete tasks more efficiently. When people say "I just did it without thinking" or "I do this automatically" one could say that they are using these habit circuits to complete the task at hand. The interesting thing about habits and behavior is that they are learned. For instance, driving at one time was a hard task to complete. It required an incredible amount of attention to focus on all the details of driving, from the traffic flow, to the speed of the car, to the feel of pressing the gas pedal and the braking distance between cars. While all of these and other details of driving are occurring, the brain is rapidly calculating what to do next. Without sufficient resources, it has to rely on making new connections. However, with more and more practice eventually these connections become "hardwired" and driving becomes a habit. Driving then becomes something that is done every day without thought, although there is a disparity between people with good driving habits and poor ones.

The same can be said of money habits—there are good money habits and poor ones. These, too, are learned habits and are taught through learned

xii

experiences such as observing how parents view, value, spend, and save money. This is where the author uses her expertise as a Certified Financial Planner to guide parents through the process of effectively teaching children money managing skills that they will use in their adult life.

MoneyBags: A Guide to Teaching Your Kids about Money is structured so that each chapter can stand alone. This provides parents with the ability to teach the lessons over a period of time rather than all at once. Each lesson can be practiced over and over to help in the establishment of good habits.

Also contributing to the formation of good habits are the meaningful and interactive conversations that will emerge with your child. The author facilitates these conversations and goes a step further by providing fun activities for you and your child to implement these new ideas into your money vernacular. Chapters like "Commit to Breaking the Cycle," "Budgeting," and "The Importance of Delayed Gratification" all provide an important foundation for children to understand the value of money, plus an entire section that focuses on "Behaviors of Good Money Managers."

Although this book is written to help parents teach their children to be effective money managers, it does not stop there, since parents learn, too, as they teach their children. They will be better able to recognize the habits in their own lives that have affected how they value and use money. By recognizing these habits and acknowledging their presence, parents will have the ability to change their own behaviors and become more effective money managers themselves.

Using the skills articulated in *MoneyBags: A Guide to Teaching Your Kids about Money*, parents and children alike will learn how to effectively recognize and learn new money behaviors. With practice and repetition, these behaviors become habits that will help our young people today—our future leaders of tomorrow—make smart values based decisions with their money and their lives.

Doug Lennick

Doug Lennick is the author of *Financial Intelligence: How to Make Smart, Values-Based Decisions with Your Money and Your Life* and *Moral Intelligence: Enhancing Business Performance and Leadership Success.*

Introduction
Living a MoneyBags Life

I remember the stories. He would count "One ... two
... three ... four ... five ... six ... SEVEN!" His favorite gimmick to drum up business was to give away free
ice cream cones to kids who had seven freckles on their
noses. His BBQ/ice cream shop called Ned's Shed was
known near and far in his day; it was impossible to not
know Ned. His imitations of the Burma Shave signs
were spaced over a mile of road; one series read, "Feel
Full ... Feel Fed ... Ned's Shed ... Dead Ahead." He
used his large white pickup with yellow running lights
as a billboard, plastering a fire-engine-red sign in the
bed of the truck, leaning against the cab that said, "Follow Me to Ned's Shed." If that didn't catch your attention, you would definitely be laughing if you saw the
black cow wearing sandwich boards with the same slo-
gan in local parades.

If you lived in the small town of Vienna, Illinois,
you likely answered your phone (whether it was your

residence, business, or you worked at the courthouse) "Let's Go to Ned's Shed!" If Ned was on the other end of the line, you could eat free for a week! It was his brainchild to call people in town randomly on Tuesday mornings between 10:00 and 10:30. If you were at the end of the party line he loved it more, since in those days up to a dozen people could pick up and listen. Imagine what he might have done with the Internet!

Ned was an honest businessman working hard to make a buck. He was a natural marketer and a shrewd investor. He was my grandfather, and I called him MoneyBags. He was an entrepreneur dabbling in businesses from Ned's Shed to a lumberyard, cattle, and his own filling station. He spent time in the navy and earned a Bachelor of Science in accounting from the University of Illinois. He was a penny pincher. The MacGyver in him was always inventing cheap, creative ways to do things. The cruise control he invented for his car used string and a clothespin clipped to a trash can sitting on the floor hump. He reused coffee grounds to save a nickel, and he could fix a hole in his pocket with a rubber band. His favorite motto was "If it's not broke, don't fix it."

Ned grew up poor and fell in love with Imogene, whose father owned a successful monument business. They lived proudly and modestly in one of the smallest houses in town, feet away from the house he grew up in, and a block away from the large, white plantation-style house where she was raised.

Coming from a long line of entrepreneurs on both sides of my father's family, I learned about money at an early age. I learned that you are guaranteed to have expenses and that your income should be valued and spent wisely. I have made it my career to help people grow their money. Daily I educate people on different products, the stock market, setting expectations, planning for uncertainty, and mostly encouraging them to save more to reach their goals by challenging their behavior.

Over the years I have noticed a pattern: most people, like me, learned about money from their parents. Hopefully, you are in the lucky pool that learned good money habits and it is your goal to be proactive in arming your kids with valuable money skills. However, there is a large part of the population that learned nothing about money from their parents. It is troubling to see the cycle being repeated through generations. If the grandparents had poor money skills or knowledge, they unknowingly kicked the can down the road as they modeled these poor money management skills to their children, who simply passed down their limited knowledge and bad habits to their children, and so on. Schools teach reading, writing, and arithmetic, but at best they only scratch the surface of money management. Imagine if, like me, your father was not a handyman. How do you learn all the "stuff" and tricks of the trade, such as "measure twice, cut once" or "righty tighty, lefty loosey," without a family teacher?

If your family happens to belong to the large pool of the population that doesn't have a good grasp on how to manage money wisely, you have to seek out the knowledge. The habits and financial blueprints are set in your children's minds at an early age, just like all the other things you teach them, such as honesty, integrity, and manners. Once your kids are behind on the financial learning curve, they will likely be playing financial catch-up for the rest of their lives.

Poor money management skills, insufficient understanding of how money works, and a lack of discipline can lead to years of frustration in trying to make ends meet—putting food on the table, covering the basic day-to-day needs, constantly trying to build an emergency fund, saving for retirement, and still wanting to enjoy the finer things in life.

I have seen the stress in peoples' lives when robbing Peter to pay Paul occurs daily. The number of people in the United States who are living paycheck to paycheck and are a pink slip away from a huge financial disaster is staggering. Poor money skills can lead to low self-esteem, shame, embarrassment, unneeded stress, late fees, low credit scores, higher interest rates, collection calls, loss of job opportunities, financial feuding with spouses, deception, divorce, and bankruptcy.

Money is seen by many people as complicated, elusive, and the root of evil. Money is none of those things. Money is just a vehicle to trade in common units. Money does not discriminate; it treats all people equally. It is like a language, but too many people are illiterate, though they deal with it every day. So, where do you go to learn about money if you did not learn good money management skills? How do you break the cycle and teach your kids the lessons you were never taught?

I have seen people receive loans to get out of a tough jam. In many cases it relieves the problem temporarily, but often another problem arises, and they are short again. Whether they finally get the job promotion or win the lottery, they have "too much month" for their money. The reality is that money, or the lack of it, is not the problem; it is a symptom. We have all heard the Chinese proverb "Give a man a fish and you feed him for a day. Teach a man to fish and you feed him for a lifetime." So let's learn how to fish!

Take the needed steps to break the cycle. Step out of your comfort zone, learn new things, try new things, change bad behaviors, and grow with your kids in discovering the joy of money. Kids are sponges for knowledge; they will learn whatever you teach them, as early as you teach them, if you break it down into terms they can understand. Give them the skills, confidence, and understanding to become financially independent. Give them a gift that they can hand down through the generations.

This book will give you the tools to:

$ Teach your kids how to manage money.

$ Learn with your kids how to eliminate bad money habits.

$ Teach your kids to spend their money wisely and save prudently for their future.

$ Eliminate the nickel and diming of your kids saying, "I want this, and I want that."

$ Have your kids respect and be responsible for things.

$ Create a new cycle of wise money management that can be passed on to future generations.

This book is designed to make it fun to teach your kids (ages five to twelve) key financial lessons so they can become financially smart and independent. This information and advice is directed to the parents (not the child). The book is not designed to be read in a couple of sittings cover to cover, but rather to be picked up and put down over time, perhaps a chapter a week. In general, the readings are short. The principles and exercises throughout the book build on earlier lessons, so going in order will work better than flipping around.

The book is in three basic parts, as follows:

1. Getting Started: This part is designed to get the ball rolling, by starting new family traditions and taking away the taboo of talking about money. This foundation provides an understanding of the difference between needs and wants. The goal is to focus on discipline and exposing your kids to money as quickly as possible so they can begin to develop an awareness of financial transactions and decision making.

2. **MoneyBags Mindset:** In any sport, two major factors create a good athlete: skills (how well one can physically perform) and behavior (mental mindset). Often people focus on the skills by practicing drills and scrimmages, but they often forget to focus on the behavior. With regard to money, people generally focus on the skills of saving, budgeting, or investing, but often overlook the behavior of managing money, which includes delayed gratification, living within your means, consistency, and avoiding temptation, such as impulse buying. Part 2 is designed to work on both skills and behavior. It teaches that it is necessary to build money, but more important to be good money managers and make good choices with money. It will help you be aware of money personalities, negative views of rich people, and learn skills that need to be ingrained in your child's mental mindset about money. It also covers the importance of following the rules, respecting things, and shopping with a purpose to propel your kids to being excellent money managers.

These behaviors can be passed down through future generations.

3. MoneyBags Mechanics: This part of the book is about the dollars and cents of how money works. It covers the value of a penny, counting money, calculating profit, the impact of stealing, the evolution of money, banking, and how credit/debit cards work.

The book's principles are short, and the exercises will be fun if you have a positive and upbeat attitude. You know your children best, so modify the practical exercises as needed to help your children understand the concepts. Enjoy the process.

Looking back at MoneyBags Moments turned this project, in part, into a look at my own upbringing. I hope that the family history and stories make you laugh, and you can learn painlessly from the book. However, please realize that this material is just one person's perspective. I am confident that you will find several good insights and ideas on how to teach your kids about money. At the end of the day, my goal is to challenge you to see and do things differently for the benefit of educating your children, so one day they can be financially independent.

PART 1
Getting Started

The Importance of Rituals

Chapter 1
Create Family Money Rituals

When I was a little kid, visiting MoneyBags and Imogene in their small hometown of Vienna, Illinois, was like being in a grown-up version of "Show and Tell." We visited all of my grandparents' siblings in town and eventually ended up at Ned's Shed for an ice-cream cone. On one trip in particular, I had a child's dilemma—my front tooth was loose and wiggly, but I was scared to have anyone pull it. I was excited because I knew the Tooth Fairy would stop by and leave me money, but I was also anxious, since my dad was dying to pull out my tooth!

While I was eating my ice cream cone, my big wiggle tooth managed to turn 180 degrees. Okay, now I was freaking out! My dad savored this moment, which felt

like a lifetime of torture, teasing me with all the painful ways he could pull out my tooth. He joked that his favorite method was to tie one end of a string around my tooth and the other end around a doorknob. Then, he could slam the door shut! With great apprehension, I listened to him explain the details as I continued to eat my ice cream. Unexpectedly, my tongue felt something hard. I looked down, and to my surprise, my tooth had fallen into my ice cream all on its own. The best part was to come. I put my tooth under my pillow that night, and the next morning I found that it had been replaced with money!

Introducing your kids to money should be fun. Creating family rituals is a great way for children to enjoy receiving cash. Receiving money is also a child's opportunity to act like an adult. In the case of the Tooth Fairy, not only are kids shedding their baby teeth; they are also making money, which is an adult-like experience. From that moment, you can begin to teach a child to save money by putting it in a safe place.

Your MoneyBags Mission

Parents, you are the creators of your family rituals. You get to decide it all. How cool! You can choose if you say a prayer, have a special box, leave a glitter trail, and so on. You can decide how much each tooth is worth via your "contract" with the Tooth Fairy, not to mention how you want to handle birthdays and other special holidays.

These rituals are opportunities to explain to your kids that money matters are private and not to be shared outside the family (see Chapter 3). For example, they should not tell their friend that they were given a dollar, because their friend may have only received fifty cents from the Tooth Fairy, since everyone has a different contract with the Tooth Fairy.

Don't stop with the Tooth Fairy and birthdays; think of other family rituals you might like to create. A wonderful children's book for ideas on creating a family tradition for lost teeth is *Throw Your Tooth on the Roof: Tooth Traditions from Around the World* by Selby B. Beeler. For other fun family rituals, read *The Book of New Family Traditions: How to Create Great Rituals for Holidays and Every Day* by Meg Cox.

Create a MoneyBags Moment today by going to the bank and getting a fifty-cent piece or a two-dollar bill, and surprise your kids with the unique present. See their joy in receiving a random gift of money and ask them what they want to do with their unexpected windfall. This is your opportunity to encourage them to save it!

Chapter 2
Family Savings Jar

One of my earliest and fondest memories related to MoneyBags and Imogene is the ugly gold-colored glass cabbage jar that sat in their living room. This jar's special purpose was to catch their loose change. The jar filled up with coins that they kept just for my sister and me. Every day they put all of their change in that jar for us. Their money habit showed me that they thought of us even when we were apart. MoneyBags and Imogene's old jar full of change was one of my earliest introductions to money. I loved counting the coins and seeing how much had accumulated. The habit of saving change is still with me; I have a loose change jar in my office that I use daily.

Teach your kids the value of little bits of money by showing them, via the Family Savings Jar, that money adds up slowly and consistently over time. Consider using the money set aside from daily loose change for some agreed-upon family goal, such as season swim passes to the local pool, money for a family trip, or a ping-pong table. Make sure that no one takes money out of the jar unless it is for the family goal.

Your MoneyBags Mission

Create a family tradition by picking out or making a container, jar, or vase to designate as your Family Savings Jar. Have it be a family event by searching in the attic or basement, going to a garage sale, or making something from scratch. In honor of MoneyBags, try to find the most outrageous, hilarious, unique savings vehicle possible—something that makes you giggle when you look at it, and is an instant conversation piece if anyone sees it. (Once you have your Family Savings Jar, please share a picture at MoneyBagslife.com.) A large piggy bank with different slots for different coins will work, or just use a reasonably sized jar. Don't go overboard by using too large of an object, such as a five-gallon water jug. Filling that might seem like an impossible task. Plus, once it is full, it will be too heavy to pick up.

Save your loose change

As soon as you have your Family Savings Jar, pick a goal for the money right away! Choosing the goal can be a fun brainstorming process for the family. Ideally, decide by a unanimous vote, so that everyone in the family can be excited about the savings goal. However, if it seems impossible to reach a consensus, go ahead and put the ideas in a hat and draw a winner, or do a simple game of rock, paper, scissors.

Place the Family Savings Jar in a prominent place in your house and toss your loose change into it daily. Have your kids count the money every three months, or more often, if your kids are really zealous. If counting money is a new or overwhelming experience, consider taking a peek at Chapter 38.

Chapter 3
Commit to Breaking the Cycle

As a Certified Financial Planner, I have noticed over the years that, for the most part, older generations disclosed little financial information to their children. Many adults know nothing about how much money their parents earned, their net worth, or how they invested their money. As their parents age, this becomes a challenging issue. Often, the first conversation about the taboo topic of finances is initiated when parents' health is declining or after they have passed away. I cannot count the number of times my clients have had to scavenge through files to try to piece together their parents' entire financial picture, not to mention the frustrating hours and money they spend trying to find detailed, comprehensive information for me, a tax advisor, or an estate attorney.

Parents are most peoples' primary source of learning about money—most people don't seek outside sources to educate themselves and money management is not taught aggressively at school. If parents don't teach their children at home, what are the odds that children will understand money and become good money managers?

Break the cycle! Begin educating your kids about money. Opening up to your kids about your financial situation is an important first step, though it can be challenging. Start slowly, to establish a comfort level for yourself and your kids. The lessons will need to be age-appropriate. Consider taking baby steps by talking to your kids and showing them small pools of money that you have, whether it is how much you carry in your wallet or purse, loose coins, or a stash of emergency cash you keep in the house. This process is not a sprint, but a marathon.

Talk to your kids about money

Your children also need to understand that this information is private and personal—not to be spoken about outside the family, with the exception of financial professionals (such as financial advisors, accountants, bankers, and estate attorneys). This is an important step in preparing your kids for responsible adulthood. They need to realize the potential dangers of the wrong person finding out too much of your financial information, such as Social Security and account numbers. They need to understand the risks of identity theft. The overall goal is to be open with them about the costs of things, purchasing decisions, your income, taxes, and your net worth (as appropriate and relevant to their ages).

Your MoneyBags Mission

As a fun starting point to change this legacy, begin by setting aside some time for a family meeting. Make a commitment to your kids that you will be open about money, and teach them at every opportunity. Make these your MoneyBags Moments. Pick a day of the week, such as Saturday morning, to work through the different passages of this book, covering topics such as savings, taxes, and good habits.

To make it official and help reinforce the importance of keeping money matters private, consider creating an agreement and having everyone in the family sign it. Go to MoneyBagsLife.com for a free turnkey agreement.

To really make it a memorable event, consider going a step further and mimic the movie *Divine Secrets of the Ya-Ya Sisterhood* by having your kids take a family oath to keep the family financial information a secret. Have fun with it! Wear crazy hats, make a bonfire, sing a song, bow, and kiss the Family Savings Jar. Unleash your creativity!

Getting Started

I [insert your name] solemnly swear [everyone put a hand on Family Savings Jar] that I will keep all family financial information private. I will only use this information for good and not bad, despite [insert the name of the biggest person in family] tickling me! I will only share our family's financial information when we need advice from outside financial professionals, since we will have so much money that we'll need their help. I realize if someone in the family slips about private information that the sacred bond will be broken and all the money in our Family Savings Jar will be given to charity. [Now, pinky swear!]

As you know, kids say the darnedest things. At some point they may slip and tell someone your financial details. They are kids, they are human, and they are learning, so they will make mistakes; we all do. Hence, you will need to keep the amount and nature of the information shared age-appropriate, continually reminding them to keep money matters private. Keep in mind that at the end of the day, the goal is to teach them about money. Ultimately, a slip means they were learning and listening, but likely got excited and forgot all the rules. When this happens, remind yourself that this is a MoneyBags Moment. It might be embarrassing, but simply pull your child aside and calmly remind them that family money topics are for family members only, "Remember the ritual and the pinky swear?" To reassert the importance of the message, follow through with the oath and go back to square one (rip up the failed agreement, decommission the Family Savings Jar, take all the saved money and give it to charity). A week later, pick out a new Family Savings Jar, create a new agreement, get crazy, and take the family oath again.

Chapter 4
Money is a Permission Item

Teach your kids that money is an extension of them. What do I mean by this? Quite simply, their money is their money. It needs to be respected as their personal property at all times. I know this may seem elementary, but I have heard stories about boundaries being crossed. The most shocking story was on an episode of the TV show *Wife Swap*. I was interested in this episode because one family was very prudent with their money and the other family was the polar opposite, spending based on whims. One example is that the father of the "spending" family bought a huge scoreboard, which was kept it in his backyard, though he had no purpose for it. He just saw it one day and purchased it because he felt it was cool and his emotions moved him. When it came time for the swap, the "saving" family's mom spent some time observing how lax the "spending" family was with their money. In one of their conversations, the "spending" father stated that when he was a little kid he had a savings account, but his parents always took money from it, so he figured, what is the point of saving if it is not respected?

Your MoneyBags Mission

Have a conversation with your kids and explain that money is a permission item. Their money is special and their ownership of it needs to be respected by everyone in the family. An analogy you can use is that your kids don't share their toothbrushes, but they do share the toothpaste. Hence, "their" money is like the toothbrush—personal. Likewise, no one should take from anyone else's piggy banks, wallets, or purses.

To start your kids off right, make sure that each child has a personal piggy bank. As a kid, I love my aunt's unique bank, an old haunted house. To deposit money, I had to place a coin in the slot on the top step in front of the door and ...wait for it... a witch would open the door and make a cackling sound, grab the coin, and scare me half to death. Go online with your kids to find the perfect bank that matches their personalities. Before you start, give your kids a limit of how much to spend and stay within that imit.

For an inexpensive option that is practical and fun to make, consider my parents' Pringles-can "piggy bank." This very special Pringles-can piggy bank, which they still keep full of money, was a craft project that one of our babysitters made with my sister and me. To make a Pringles-can bank, simply give your kids permanent markers to draw pictures on newspaper or construction paper. Once done, cut the paper to the appropriate size and tape the paper onto the can. Then, with scissors or a knife, carefully cut a slot in the lid large enough for quarters and, *PRESTO!* You have a piggy bank.

To make this event a big deal, consider priming your child's new piggy bank with the gift of a dollar. Another fun option is to create a money hunt game, similar to an Easter egg hunt. Throughout your house, simply hide loose change. Put a penny by the dog bowl, a quarter by the fish tank, a nickel in the fruit basket, and so on. If you have multiple children and you feel it is important to keep the money found equal, give each child a room to search and hide the same amount of money in each room. Go a step further like Meg Cox reveals in her book *The Book of New Family Traditions: How to Create Great Rituals for Holidays and Every Day* by "Celebrating with a Burst." Purchase packets of balloons and put a coin or bill into each balloon before you inflate them. For safety reasons and quick cleanup, place the balloons in a room free of furniture and let your kids pop them to find the money surprises.

> **Note:** *You will want your kids to have three savings vehicles, which will be discussed in greater detail in Chapter 10. Make sure this special piggy bank is earmarked for MoneyBags Savings. Consider plainer options for the other saving vehicles.*

The Big Picture

Chapter 5
Needs versus Wants

I have an adorable client whom I truly love. In a meeting one day, she had me on the floor laughing as she explained in all seriousness that she and her husband HAD to buy a new pontoon boat. It was a NEED since they live on a lake. She was totally convinced this was a NEED, therefore, I should not question their purchasing decision. As she was going through a long explanation, her husband sat quietly chuckling since he knew I was going to challenge her on the difference between a NEED and a WANT.

In economics, a NEED is something you cannot live without, such as food, water, air, and shelter. A WANT is anything else. I have placed this lesson in the front of the book since I feel like it is ground zero for making good money decisions. The first step in good money management is knowing the difference between NEEDs and WANTs.

Your MoneyBags Mission

Explain to your kids that NEEDs are the basic things you need to live (food, water, air, and shelter) and everything else is a WANT.

Talk to your kids about your family or neighbor's pet and ask these questions:

- $ Does it NEED or WANT water?
- $ Does it NEED or WANT a chew toy?
- $ Does it NEED or WANT food?
- $ Does it NEED or WANT a haircut?
- $ Does it NEED or WANT a warm, dry place to sleep?
- $ Does it NEED or WANT a diamond-studded collar?

Over the next month, when you go to the store and your kids say they NEED something, challenge them by asking if they really NEED it, or do they WANT it?

Chapter 6
Maslow's Hierarchy of Needs

It is impossible to talk about needs and wants without referring to Maslow's Hierarchy of Needs.[1] His theory states that a pecking order of needs provides the motivations behind all human behavior; the first and lowest level is your Physiological Needs (food, water, air, and shelter). This is the caveman level: the need to survive. Your entire existence depends on finding food, water, air to breathe, and shelter from the elements. Once you have found your cave and sources of food and water, your baseline needs are covered. You now enter a new level of needs.

The second level is Safety and Security Needs (protection, order, and stability). In caveman world, you need to make sure that your cave will not collapse,

---

1. *Consumer Behavior* by Leon G Schiffman and Leslie Lazar Kanuk, pps 97-99.

remains clean, and will not be attacked by animals. This is the nesting level. You have a home to go to so you can drop your club. At this point you are a skilled hunter, and the number of times you come home without food is minimal, so you are confident that you will eat daily. You set up booby traps to prevent predator animals or unwelcome cavemen from entering and taking over your cave when you are out hunting.

Once the Safety and Security Needs are met, you proceed to the Social Needs Level (affection, friendship, and belonging). At this level, you look for people like you. You search for a spouse and want to have a family. You feel the need to live in a community and learn how to communicate. To satisfy your social needs, you find a spouse, have kids, hang out with the tribe, and create cave drawings.

The fourth level is Ego Needs (prestige, status, and self-esteem). This level is where competition comes in. As a caveman, you want the largest animal head trophy, fur, and enough meat to feed the tribe for a month. You manage to find and support a second cave home with another tribe. You are proud to produce the most children and send them five tribes away to learn exotic cave drawings. This is the fun level.

The last tier is Self-Actualization (self-fulfillment). This level is only possible when the other levels are met and relates to fulfilling your potential as a person. You have accepted your past, your flaws, and your uniqueness. You tend to have a deep understanding of others, your own nature, and you are comfortable with solitude. As a self-actualized caveman, you look back on your life and feel content. Buying a birthday present for you is difficult since you have everything you need and want. You have found inner peace and are happy with things in your life, like family, health, and the predictability of the sun rising in the east. You have achieved your goals and found meaning in life. You have found inner peace, and you are happy.

Throughout life, you will always have a quest to climb and fulfill a need at a higher level, but if at any time one of the lower-level needs, such as hunger, is not met, you must step back and fulfill it.

Your MoneyBags Mission

For fun, have everyone in the family make a list of their needs and their wants. Notice, everyone should have the same NEEDs, but once you reach the WANTs you will likely see a large difference in family members' goals. When listing your WANTs, encourage your kids to go wild dreaming about what they want. Remember, dreaming is free!

Consider mimicking Meg Cox's *The Book of New Family Traditions: How to Create Great Rituals for Holidays and Every Day* by creating "Balloon Wishes." Simply have your child write three of their biggest wants or dreams on a piece of paper and tie them to their own individual helium-filled balloon. With closed eyes and a kiss, have your kids make a wish as they release their balloons. Let their dreams float up to the sky to symbolize the unlimited potential of their dreams coming true.

Another option to consider is to making a family time capsule and placing the family wants in an envelope. Then select something that is not opened often, such as their baby book, family photo album, tackle box, or junk drawer (in my family, it would be the tool box). Later, when you stumble upon it, read the list out loud as a family. Have your kids' wants changed over time? Have fun updating the list and re-hide it until the next time you stumble upon it.

Chapter 7
The Money Hierarchy

The Money Hierarchy is based on Maslow's Hierarchy of Needs. You need to satisfy the first level of needs before fully graduating to the next level. It is likely that your life straddles two levels, but you cannot fully graduate to the next level until you have completed the needs on the lower level. I view the Money Hierarchy like a cake.

The Plate Level

The lowest level of the Money Hierarchy is the "plate," since it is the foundation for your cake. When it comes to money, you want to ensure you have a good, solid plate that will support your cake. If you have a cracked or chipped plate, it is like being unemployed or living paycheck to paycheck. The money you have

is short or barely meeting your basic needs. It is not reliable, and you have no savings, which causes stress. When your plate is cracked you are always robbing Peter to pay Paul. Hence, you need to fix the problem before you can graduate to the next level. To strengthen your plate or repair any cracks in the foundation, you may need to change careers, go back to school, and/or reduce your expenses. At this stage, it is important to look at the big picture of what you want and take the needed steps to make your long-term vision work. In other words, short-term pain for long-term gain.

The Ingredients Level

The second level is the "ingredients." If you are missing ingredients, it's hard to make a good cake. At this level, your need for savings and insurance comes into play. If you don't have the needed ingredients for your cake, it will threaten your ability to stay at this level and advance to the higher ones. Any chef will tell you that missing key ingredients will ruin your cake.

Good ingredients equal protection. Protection is a key ingredient. You need to protect your income (emergency funds/disability insurance), protect your health (medical insurance), protect your family (life insurance/basic estate planning), protect your house (homeowners insurance/maintenance), protect your car (auto insurance/repairs), and ensure you are able to adapt and survive changes to your environment (education).

The Ingredients Level requires spending money on important things, not the "fun stuff." Many people feel that they are invincible, so why should they spend money on insurance? Insurance is expensive in their eyes, since they are only thinking short-term. In other words, why pay $3,000 a year for medical insurance when I am healthy? Well, today they are healthy, but what about tomorrow? Have you ever noticed how many people don't want to pay for insurance, but when something goes wrong they feel someone else should pay? Ironically, many people only think insurance is a good idea once they become uninsurable and no one will sell them insurance (i.e., they have terminal cancer and now they want to purchase life insurance). Consider this the "Murphy's Law Effect"—if you buy the insurance, you won't need it. If only that was a guarantee. Conversely, what if you did need the insurance? If you have the insurance, then you are covered. Whew!

This level is also where you protect your dream of eventually reaching the Cherry-on-Top Level: retirement/financial independence. To protect your retirement dream, you need to begin "gathering ingredients" by establishing retirement savings (i.e., saving into a retirement plan, such as an IRA, 401(k), or 403(b)). At the very least, make sure to save enough to receive 100% of any employer match or, if you don't have an employer plan, just start saving 2–5% of your income to an Individual Retirement Account (IRA). To graduate to the next level, you need to have proper insurance in place, emergency funds established (three to six months of living expenses), and retirement savings started.

The Cake Level

The third level is where the "cake" comes in. Fun enters the picture, and you can lick the bowl. You have good discretionary income, and you are able to save for a future car purchase, house down payment, and/ or college education. You can enjoy things like going to the movies, cable TV, dinners out, theater, nicer furniture, and "stuff." This is where you can enjoy planning and saving for vacations. This is also the level where, if you are charitably inclined, you can begin giving money and time. In order to advance to the next level, your retirement savings plan is funded beyond the government's maximum allowable savings limits (i.e., in 2013 the maximum you can save to a 401(k) plan is $17,500 and, if you are fifty years old or older, a $5,500 catch-up contribution). At this point, if you have not already done so, consider hiring a Certified Financial Planner to help you graduate to the higher levels.

The Icing Level

Fittingly, the Icing Level is what Maslow calls the Ego Needs Level. At this stage of the financial game, everything is pacing well and you are on track to reach the top level. You have no debt, unless it is structured wisely. You can afford to buy luxury items, though you may opt not to. These may include crazy expensive birthday parties, an in-home theater, designer clothes, expensive jewelry, live-in help (nanny, chef, house-keeper), yachts, expensive cars, a cabin or lake home, a second residence, private education for your kids, first-class travel, and more. This is what many think of as the "good stuff." Life is good. You are able to enjoy the fruits of your labor and purchase things you want. To graduate to the next level, you must be financially independent.

The Cherry-on-Top Level

The Self-Actualization Level is reaching retirement or financial independence! This IS the "Cherry on Top"! This level is attained when you have saved enough money that you don't need a paycheck from an employer. You have a few different ways to reach this level. The traditional way is to limit spending, keep your expenses low, aggressively save, and invest your money wisely. Your other option is to find a way to have such a large stream of money coming in each month (like Oprah) that you can easily cover all levels of needs, save money, enjoy the Icing Level, and be financially independent.

According to Maslow, most people don't reach the top level of Self-Actualization, and this is also true for financial independence. When it comes to money, some people never get to the ingredients level and saving for retirement. Others jump to or get stuck on the Icing Level. When people jump to the Icing Level prematurely or stay there too long, enjoying the shiny new things, they can enter into a kind of "sugar high." The Icing Level is a test. In order to graduate to the top level, you have to forego temptations. For many people, every time they enjoy something at the Icing Level, they fall a few steps back from the top tier, due to the cash outlay, and the cherry moves further way.

Be aware that many people believe that those who are financial free are "lucky." Well, they may have had some luck, but most people who attain this level do so due to discipline and good decision making. When you reach the Cherry-on-Top Level, be proud of your accomplishments and the decisions you made to get there. It took great disciple to save and/or forego purchases. You may have chosen to work two jobs or get a higher education to increase your income potential. Maybe you chose to: have only two kids instead of four, drive your cars into the ground, go camping versus taking expensive vacations, avoid purchasing expensive toys (four wheelers, boats, jet skis, trampolines, or snowmobiles), or lived in a modest house to keep your expenses low.

Your MoneyBags Mission

Take a step back to reflect and think about what level of the Money Hierarchy you are on. Do you like your current level? Do you feel you are going in the right direction? Do you need to focus and make changes to get to the next level? Have you jumped levels without fully completing others?

Consider walking your kids through the different levels and letting them know which level you are on. Tell your kids the steps the family needs to take to get to the next level, such as going back to school, purchasing insurance, saving more money, paying down debt, and so on. You will be amazed how much kids want to help the family move forward. Doing this makes them feel like part of the team and like they can help contribute to reaching the family goal. If you are cutting out cable, consider replacing it with game night. If you are planning to limit eating out, replace it with awesome family dinners. It is important to do what you say you will do. If you tell your kids you are cutting out cable so you can build cash reserves, but then you turn around and purchase an expensive cell phone, your kids will see the disconnect.

As a family, think about the Money Hierarchy. Do you know people who own smart phones and fully loaded cable television, but don't save for retirement? Do you know someone who drives a really expensive truck, but doesn't have the ability to comfortably absorb the cost of gas going up to five dollars a gallon or cover the expense for new tires? Do you know of someone who is house poor? This occurs when their home has more space than they can afford to furnish, or when replacing a roof is outside of their means. How about people who always have their nails manicured and tan regularly, but don't have medical insurance? In recent years the stock and housing markets crashed, the economy slowed, and unemployment entered double digits. This really damaged some people and pulled them down a few levels, but is it also possible that some people jumped to the Icing Level and failed to ensure that they had good ingredients for their cake? Was their plate chipped?

Pivotal Changes

Chapter 8
The Importance of Discipline

"Talent without discipline is like an octopus on roller skates. There's plenty of movement, but you never know if it's going to be forward, backward, or sideways."
—H. Jackson Brown Jr.

"Discipline is the bridge between goals and accomplishment."
—Jim Rohn

"Self-respect is the fruit of discipline; the sense of dignity grows with the ability to say no to oneself."
—Abraham Joshua Heschel

"The more disciplined you become, the easier life gets."
—Steve Pavlina

Discipline. Many people attach a negative connotation to the word *discipline*, despite the fact that it is a required ingredient to attain one's goals. Being an Olympian, writer, president, teacher, doctor, dancer, singer, or awesome parent requires discipline. If you want to succeed in the money game, you must have discipline. Discipline is simply exercising self-control to meet personal goals by forgoing temptations that distract from the accomplishment of the goal. Discipline is teachable, since you can practice and train to improve your self-control.

Under the glass on my desk, I have the quotation, "Choose discipline or choose regret." The saying stems from the book *Conversations with Millionaires: What Millionaires Do to Get Rich, That You Never Learned About in School* by Mike Litman and Jason Oman. In their book, they state, "We suffer one of two things. Either the pain of discipline or the pain of regret. You've got to choose discipline versus regret. Because discipline weighs ounces and regret weighs tons." Take a minute to really think about that concept. This not only applies to money, but all things.

Choose discipline or choose regret

My favorite story of unwavering discipline is about Milo of Croton, a legendary sixth-century BCE wrestler. As a young boy, he trained for the Olympics by picking up a calf every day as they both grew. By the time Milo was a teenager, he could carry the full-grown bull on his shoulders. Legend has it that he entered his first Olympic event with a bull over his shoulders as he walked across the Olympic track. The only way Milo was able to do this was due to his unwavering discipline in lifting the calf every day.

If you can teach your children to be disciplined in reaching their goals, the possibilities are endless. For them to be successful personal money managers, teach your kids the discipline of saving money. Continue to commit to them by being disciplined and working through all the chapters in this book.

Your MoneyBags Mission

One way to practice self-control is to make a conscious decision to give something up for a specified period of time. This is practiced in some religions where followers choose to forgo something they enjoy for forty days.

For fun and to practice discipline, for the next forty days have everyone in the family give up something that they enjoy (chocolate, ice cream, potatoes, coffee, skateboarding, TV, or texting) or commit to a new routine, such as completing homework right after school or going to the gym in the morning. Whatever you decide to give up or commit to, consider it the "temptation." Use a calendar to count down the days by having your child write forty, thirty-nine, thirty-eight, and so on as each day passes. This will help them lock in success and see the light at the end of the tunnel. You can also take it a step further and mark a day with an "X" if someone slipped that day. If someone does slip, don't shame them for giving into temptation, but keep working with them on their personal control. Explore why they slipped (peer pressure, they forgot, or ran into trouble finding a substitute) and help them come up with strategies to overcome their obstacles.

Keep the following in mind as you work through the exercise above.

$ When choosing the temptation you are planning to avoid or the commitment you are making for forty days, make sure you are very clear. Is it carbohydrates or only bread? Getting to the gym in the morning or any form of exercise?

$ If you are aware that discipline is a struggle in your family, consider easing into it, so you can find success. For example, consider initially trying the exercise for a week. Then a month later, try it again for two weeks. Then, a couple of months later, commit to thirty days. Then wait a while and complete forty days.

$ If someone gives up a temptation that costs money, such as daily coffee at the local coffee shop, consider putting the money saved into the Family Savings Jar (Chapter 2).

Once the forty days are up, as a family, answer the following questions.

$ When you succeeded in avoiding the temptation or keeping to your commitment, how did it feel to be true to your word?

$ After forty days, was the sacrifice or commitment a big deal? Was it hard to do?

$ Do you feel a sense of accomplishment and control over your actions?

$ How does it feel to reintroduce the temptation or drop the commitment and bring your life back to normal? Have you decided to stay disciplined?

$ If you slipped, how did you feel? Did you have regret? Was buckling to the temptation or skipping your commitment as joyful as you thought it would be? What made you weak?

Consider doing this exercise as a family every year to practice discipline.

Chapter 9
The Importance of Giving an Allowance

My parents started giving my sister and me an allowance at an early age. We had baseline chores (clean our bedrooms, set and clear the table, put dishes in the dishwasher, and so on) that needed to be completed in order to earn our allowance. My mom was consistent. Like clockwork, we always received our allowance every Saturday morning. We never had to ask her; it was always sitting on our placemats as part of our Saturday morning breakfast routine. I loved getting my money and, of course, saving it! I loved to count it and put it into my piggy bank. I never knew what I was saving it for. I just loved watching it grow (can you imagine my joy when I found out about interest?).

It is important to give your kids an allowance, and start early. You win in several ways. First, they learn about money. They can touch it and feel it. You should give them actual cash versus creating a credit system that is tracked on paper (see Chapter 12). They need to learn how to be responsible by keeping track of it. By having their very own special piggy bank, they now have a place to put it.

They also have to choose what they do with their money; do they spend it or save it? They will learn how it feels to lose money or be swindled out of it by a bigger kid. Plus, they will likely learn about lending money by making occasional deals with their siblings. Once your kids have an allowance, you can have them use their money to buy items they want. This is a great tool if you run into "I want this" or "I want that" when you go shopping. Suddenly, kids don't want to part with their own money. They also learn about purchasing mistakes. When they have some skin in the game, they care a little more when a toy is broken or lost.

Lastly, when you give your kids an allowance, you have a new tool to discipline them. For example, if they tend to swear or behave poorly, reduce or eliminate their allowance for that week, based on the severity of their behavior. Ideally, use this as a last resort, to show severity, since you want the payment of allowance tied to the completion of their chores.

There are two common ways that giving an allowance becomes ineffective. The first way is when your kids don't receive it regularly. When you don't give an allowance consistently, your kids will not take it seriously, because you don't. Second, if you keep buying them everything they want, many kids will stop doing their baseline chores. They figure, why work for money when I get everything I want anyway? Be prepared, if you have always said yes to your kids and stop doing so, you will see resistance. This is especially true if you are starting an allowance with an older child.

Your MoneyBags Mission

Choose an age-appropriate allowance to give your kids. A common rule of thumb is one dollar per year of age per week. For example, if you have an eight-year-old and a five-year-old, consider giving your older child $8 weekly and your younger child $5 weekly for their allowance. If this is too steep, choose an amount you can consistently give them.

It is important that they have enough money to buy a few things they want, but not so much that they can get everything on their wish list and more. In other words, they need to be short so they have an incentive to spend their money wisely. This also becomes your cue to stop paying for everything.

Tell your children that receiving their allowance is their first job. Explain to them that doing their baseline chores is a job and payday is on Friday (or whatever day you choose, but keep it consistent like your employer does). If they don't do their job, you will dock their pay. It is important to be consistent, so I recommend keeping a stash of cash (small bills and coins) at your house in a safe or secure place, so that you have cash on hand.

On your child's birthday, make it a big deal that they are getting another dollar a week! It is a raise just like they would receive for seniority at a union job, or you can explain that their birthday is their annual review, so they are getting a raise for their hard work. At this time, consider adding more responsibility since they have more pay, or explain that certain jobs earn them bonus money, such as mowing the lawn, shoveling snow, walking the dog, or babysitting.

Meg Cox's book, *The Book of New Family Traditions: How to Create Great Rituals for Holidays and Every Day*, has a great birthday ritual that she calls "Celebrate Growth." To complement the raise, give your child two envelopes, one marked "New Privilege" and the other marked "New Responsibility." The new privilege could be moving bedtime later by a half hour, and the responsibility could be feeding the family pet.

A fun game to play that lets your young kids start experiencing money is "The Allowance Game" by Lakeshore Learning. This game allows young kids to handle play money as they work their way around the game board. As they move their game pieces over the board, they are rewarded for work, such as mowing the lawn and babysitting, or they will land on a space that costs them money, such as purchasing a teddy bear or playing video games. As they pass Home they collect their allowance, which gets them closer to their goal of being the first player to earn and save twenty dollars. I would suggest a couple of enhancements to the rules to make it more accurate and a better experience. (For a free download of recommended rule changes, go to MoneyBagsLife.com.)

$ When your kids make a deposit to the bank, have them collect interest every time they pass the space versus only when they land on the space.

$ If someone lands on the Lemonade Stand space and it has an owner, have the buyer roll the dice to determine how many cups to purchase from the owner.

Chapter 10
SAVE . . . Taxes . . . Share . . . Spend

When I fly, I always think of money when I hear the safety speech. They always say to "please securely place your oxygen mask on first, before helping others." Why do they say that? Simple, if you don't get your mask on, you become the next problem. However, if you put your mask on first, even before your child, then not only can you not help your child, but other people who may be struggling. Money is the same way!

Many people think it's selfish to put themselves before others when it comes to money. Some people have misinterpreted religious teachings, thinking they need to give away all their money (oxygen). I disagree. I do feel you should give to charities and worthy causes, as long as you are financially secure, which starts with paying yourself first. Down the road, you can help even more people, instead of becoming someone who needs help. If you only have $100 in your savings account, how many people can you help without taking yourself down in the process?

However, if you have amassed $1,000,000 in a savings account making a modest 1% a year simple interest ($1,000,000 x .01 = $10,000), you can take the $10,000 annually and help more people than you could with the $100 in your savings account. Furthermore, you will not risk becoming one who needs financial help.

Give your kids the gift of learning how hard it is to build up money and how easy it is to spend

Moreover, you may be able to retire early and dedicate the remainder of your life to giving back via service, using the very skills that created your wealth. Plus, you can leave all your money to charity upon your death. Another way to look at giving to charity is that you can always give two ways, time or money. If you are low on money, find ways to give your time.

In his book, *Prodigal Sons and Material Girls: How Not to Be Your Child's ATM*, Nathan Dungan suggests teaching your kids how to handle their money via "Share Save Spend." He is close, but I have added two twists. As a Certified Financial Planner, I have to laugh at the contradiction in my industry. We always preach "pay yourself first." However, most budget sheets list savings as the last line item. To get your kids trained right, teach them SAVE/Taxes/Share/Spend with their allowance. Once you have decided on the amount of your children's allowance, proceed to guide them in how to handle their money. To keep it easy, designate their allowance as shown below. To drive this lesson home, make sure they see you practice with them. This is the first step to teaching budgeting and discipline.

SAVE: MoneyBags Savings (25%)

Teach your kids to ALWAYS pay themselves first by putting 25% of their money into their special and unique piggy bank (Chapter 4). For example, when they receive $10, have them earmark $2.50 ($10 x .25 = $2.50). Don't hesitate because it is not a round dollar amount; stay firm. If your 401(k) plan can handle the odd amounts, so can you and your kids. The money that goes into this pool is not to be spent for several— ten or more— years. If you do it right, this pool of money could help them with college costs, a car purchase, a house down payment, or an emergency fund, as a result of their good habits. Once they enter the working world, this good habit will fund their retirement savings.

Note: *If you think this is too much to earmark for long-term savings, here's the math. If you start your child's allowance at age five ($5 a week) and stop on their eighteenth birthday, with a dollar raise* *on their birthdays, they will have $1,872, excluding interest.*

Taxes: Family Tax Kitty (25%)

Only two things are certain in life: death and taxes. The sooner you teach your kids about taxes, the better. Explain to your kids that you pay taxes directly out of your paycheck, which goes to both the state and federal government for many important services and benefit programs. Since your children are part of the family and live under your roof, they are gaining protection and other services. For this fourth of your kids' money, consider creating a Family Tax Kitty to pool these funds. Use this pool of money at your discretion when the family has a need, such as house or car repairs. Make sure your kids are aware of what you are using this pool of money for, so they can see their "tax" money used for the overall good of the family. (See Chapter 11 for more details.)

Share: Charity (10%)

Consider earmarking 10% of your kids' money for charity. The goal is for your child to learn about sharing and giving back to others. Have fun with how you want to handle this pot of money. If you go to church regularly, this can simply be the money they put into the offering plate. Another option is to be spontaneous: pay it forward by buying lunch for the people behind you in the drive-thru, or put it in a Salvation Army kettle. To increase your children's passion, have them pick a charity that they can connect to, such as the Animal Humane Society.

Spend: Fun Stuff (40%)

This portion of your kids' money comes last, but it is important. The reason they work so hard is to enjoy the fruits of their labor. This is the reward. If your kids want a toy or a cell phone, this is the pool of money that needs to build for them to make the purchase. Give your kids the gift of learning how hard it is to build money and how quick and easy it is to spend it. By letting them work to build the money, they WILL respect it more.

When your child starts to build money for a goal, make sure to record the goal and the date started. If it takes fifteen weeks to save up the money, make sure you praise your child's accomplishment. Then, to show how fast and easy it is to spend money, time how quickly the transaction occurs at the register. Make this a Money-Bags Moment by reinforcing with your children that it took fifteen weeks of disciplined savings to build up enough money for their goal and less than a minute to spend it.

Finally, in regard to your child's allowance, there are three things to note. First, as your children save money for their spending goals, it is all right for them to change the goal. For example, if your child is saving for a toy and then wants to change it to a skateboard, that's okay. Second, don't limit this discipline of allocating into four buckets to your child's allowance; implement it for all the money that they receive, including babysitting, mowing lawns, gifts, or part-time jobs. Third, if they have a job that withholds taxes, skip putting money in the Family Tax Kitty since taxes were already taken out of their paycheck.

Your MoneyBags Mission

Create a system to set aside money in these four buckets via piggy banks, jars, or envelopes. You will need to create a Family Tax Kitty, so this is a great way to introduce the new system to your kids. Have a fun family meeting and explain that, like you, they need to allocate money to the different buckets. Let your kids know about taxes. Tell them this is how they pay for their "family benefits," such as food, shelter, education, and protection, not to mention taxi service. Clearly label the different pots of money. Be aware that clear containers allow your kids to see the money and watch it build toward their goals. On the other hand, non-transparent banks help keep the money out of sight and out of mind.

If you are comfortable with this idea, pull out your paycheck stub and show your kids your gross pay, your contribution to your retirement plan (401(k)/403(b) plan, etc.), your withholding for taxes, and your net pay. Show them if you have an automatic deposit to your checking and/or savings accounts. If you are not saving money to a retirement plan, go ahead and show your kids. Then, commit to your kids that you will go into work the next day and enroll in your employer's retirement plan. Make sure the percentage you save maximizes any employer match. For example, if your employer matches 50% of your contribution on the first 4% (a total of 2%), then you need to save 4% to capture all the free money your employer provides. If your employer does not have a retirement plan, don't let that stop you; go ahead and systematically save to an Individual Retirement Account (IRA). If you are uncomfortable disclosing this much information to your kids, then consider making the amount $1,000, as an example, and tell them the percentages that goes to each area.

Monthly, have your child count and track the money they have in their MoneyBags Savings (see Chapter 38). Consider tracking their growth by using construction paper and creating a chart with months on the bottom axis and dollars on the vertical axis. Another fun way to track the growth of their savings is on their height chart. When you measure their height, also record the amount in their MoneyBags Savings!

Chapter 11
Taxes

One beautiful summer day, I was sitting in a boat on a lake, enjoying the peaceful rocking with my friend and her family. This was the last place I thought I would learn about money, but I did, and I laugh every time I think of it. My girlfriend's daughter Bridget (age 6) was hungry, so she asked her mom, Ali, for a sandwich. Sure enough, Ali, who is also in the money business, pulled the sandwich out of the cooler, took it out of its little plastic baggie, and just before she handed it over to Bridget took a HUGE bite out of it. Bridget's priceless response was, "I know Mommy—taxes."

Taxes! Ask anyone and they will almost always cringe when you start talking about taxes. Often you hear people complain about paying taxes, but it does not mean that taxes are bad. Taxes actually serve an important function in our day-to-day lives. So, what are taxes? Taxes are simply a financial fee, based on one's income or purchases (sales tax), that everyone has to pay to raise money for basic services such as schools, roads, sewers, jails, and libraries, and benefit programs like Social Security, unemployment, Medicare, and Medicaid.

The way income taxes work is that everyone is required to pay a percentage of their income to the government for these services. For example, in allowance terms, if the tax rate is 10% and your children's allowance is $10, then they owe $1 to the government. It is important to know that in general, the amount of taxes you pay is determined by two things. First, the percentage you are required to pay is determined by the government; over time, the percentage goes up and down. The second is based on your income. In the simplest of terms, assume everyone is taxed a flat 25%. If you make $10,000, your tax bill is $2,500 ($10,000 x 0.25 = $2,500). Consequently, if you make $40,000, you will pay the same percentage of tax, but you now owe $10,000 ($40,000 x 0.25 = $10,000). Similarly, if the government raises taxes to 30%, the person making $10,000 now owes $3,000 in taxes ($10,000 x 0.3 = $3,000) and the person making $40,000 now owes $12,000 ($40,000 x 0.3 = $12,000). So, if your children's allowance is $10 and the tax is 30%, they now owe the Family Tax Kitty $3 ($10 x 0.3 = $3).

Your MoneyBags Mission

To give your kids a hands-on experience of where their taxes go, consider a field trip to the local fire station, police station, library, or park. Explain that everyone's tax money goes toward funding these services for the community.

When you go on an errand run, have your kids write down or call out all the things they see that exist because of taxes. After your outings, show your children the receipts from items purchased and look at what percentage was paid in sales tax. Have your kids track money spent on taxes for a month by collecting all your receipts. With your kids, evaluate the taxes paid. Is the percentage of tax the same for food and clothing? Does the percentage of tax vary from city to city? Have your kids tally the amount of money spent on taxes for the month. Then, have your kids multiply that amount by twelve to find your estimated sales tax for the year.

For fun, consider going a step further by going online and looking up the federal income tax rate tables for this year. Depending on your comfort level, have your children locate your highest income tax bracket and the rate at which are you taxed.

Chapter 12
The Value of a Dollar: Begin Using ONLY Cash

I remember driving up to my mother's parents' house in Chicago when I was a kid. Going from the country to the suburbs, many things were different, such as the taste of the water. My mother explained the reason that the water tasted so odd was because they had well water. With my Southern accent and no understanding of what a well was, I interpreted that to mean that a whale lived under their house. I am not sure how she missed the confused look on my face, but it happened. So, for a couple of years I wondered how the whale stayed alive out of the ocean. How did they put it under the house? Did it have a name? Could I go look at it? How did it know when to shoot its water up on command?

I tell you this story to remind you that even though you explain something to your kids, you might not have a meeting of the minds, especially with an intangible subject like money. It is likely that your kids have no idea where money comes from or the difference between $1 and $1,000,000 any more than Dustin Hoffman's character Raymond Babbitt did in the movie *Rain Man*. In the movie, Tom Cruise's character, Charlie Babbitt, discovers that his brother Ray, who has autism, has a unique ability to count and do math in his head lightning-fast, with the accuracy of a calculator.

Begin only using cash

Charlie is amazed, and during their long trip across the country, he finally takes Ray to see a small-town doctor for an evaluation. The doctor explains that even though Ray is a genius with numbers, he has no concept of how much things cost. Ray could accurately complete a complicated math problem in a split second, but if you asked him how much a candy bar or car cost, he would say $100.

To kids, money must seem like magic. Most people have their paycheck directly deposited into their checking accounts. We enjoy the convenience of automated payments for mortgages, car loans, and multiple bills. It has also become more convenient to use credit and debit cards to make purchases. Plus, there are these awesome machines that you put a plastic card into and it spits out cash!

To help you and your kids have a meeting of the minds when it comes to money, you need to teach them the value of a dollar and how much things cost. As you do this, watch for confused looks on their faces and make sure to have them explain things back to you in their own words.

Your MoneyBags Mission

To help your kids visualize money, consider making a conscious choice to begin only using cash around your kids. This will allow them to see physical money, so they have a better feel for the process versus the magical swipe of a debit or credit card. Using cash will help them, and it is an excellent exercise for you. Plus, this practice will create more change daily for your Family Savings Jar. To start, determine how much money you spend when you are with your children (gas, groceries, dining out, entertainment, and so on). Every week, go with your kids to the bank or your automatic teller machine (ATM) and withdraw the needed cash.

Another fun way to help your kids gain a better feel for the cost of things is to make a game of it. Play your own version of *The Price Is Right's* "High Low" game. Simply point to different things around the house and ask your kids how much they cost. For example, point to your couch and ask your kids how much you paid. Let's assume you paid $2,500. If they say $5, tell them higher; if they say $1,000,000 say lower, and so on.

Help them understand correlations that drive up or lower the cost, such as size, weight, technology, brand names, and whether something is handmade or mass produced. This can also be a fun game when you are out shopping.

Another way to teach your kids the value of a dollar is to break it down into terms they can understand, such as their allowance. If their allowance is $10 a week and they want a $150 cell phone, explain to them how many weeks they have to save 40% of their allowance for the cell phone. For example, "So you really like this cell phone? It costs $150 plus 6% tax ($150 x .06 = $9, $9 + $150 = $159) for a total of $159. Do you realize that you will have to save 40% of your money ($10 x .40 = $4) for the next 40 weeks straight ($159 / $4 = 39.75 weeks, 39.75 / 4 weeks per month = 9.975 months) before you will have enough money to buy the cell phone? In other words, it will take almost 10 months. If you start saving in January, you will meet your goal in October."

When you go out to dinner, pump gas, buy groceries, or go to the movies, constantly ask your kids how many weeks they would have to save 40% of their allowance (or how many hours they would have to work at their part-time jobs) before they could afford to make the purchase themselves. For example, if a tank of gas cost $40, plus 5% tax ($40 x .05 = $2, $2+ $40 = $42) and your child's allowance is $5 a week, then they need 21 weeks of allowance money saved before they can buy that tank of gas ($5 x .40 spend = $2, $2 / $42 = 21weeks, 21 / 4 = 5.25 months).

Chapter 13
You Need to Say NO

I went to church one day and the pastor hit on a hot topic. Tell your kids, "I love you—NO." NO was a word in my parents' vocabulary. Like all kids, I was often mad that they would tell me NO. However, now I am grateful. It taught me that in life you don't get *everything* you want, which is okay. I learned that I would live, and just maybe that thing I wanted so much was not good for me. Saying NO is hard for so many people since they are concerned that their kids will not like them and, in the short-term, it is easier to say YES than to deal with the outcome of a NO response.

In teaching your kids how to be good stewards of money, it is important to tell them NO when you go shopping. I have seen many people in the trap of always saying YES to their kids. It is vital to say NO since you are the one in control of the family budget. Kids can nickel and dime you to death. If kids' "I want this and

I want that" drives the family out of budget and into a deficit, whose fault is it? The parents' or the children's? Hands down, it is the parents' fault if the budget runs into a deficit. You are in charge of the family finances. Don't let your children drive you. In order to succeed, you must say NO.

Be aware that your kids have learned the "Ten Commandments," as noted in Nathan Dungan's book *Prodigal Sons and Material Girls: How Not to Be Your Child's ATM*. The first commandment is—"Nag and You Shall Receive," and if you don't get what you want, throw a tantrum. There are nine more commandments, so you might want to read his book and learn what they are, so you can be ready!

Your MoneyBags Mission

When you go shopping, start by communicating to your kids that you are going to the store with your shopping list and only buying what's on it. If they pick up something and ask you to buy it, remind them that they WANT it and that it is not on your list. If it is candy, explain it is not healthy food; if it is a cheap toy, explain it will likely break; if it is expensive, tell them it is too much. Remind them that you are going off your shopping list only, and to stop asking. Tell them to make a list and write it down as a WANT for their birthday or Christmas. Moreover, it is important not to use the excuse that you are broke or poor. To your kids, this

You Need to Say NO

means: IF you had money, you would buy it. You want them to know the answer is NO and even IF you had the money, the answer would still be NO.

Over the next couple of weeks, consider having fun saying NO like a bit on my local radio station KDWB's *The Dave Ryan Show*: "Steve-O Teaches Your Kids the Meaning of NO." Steve-O is a new father practicing how to say NO to his daughter. The bit entails tween girls calling into the station asking him for Justin Bieber tickets (or whatever). His job is to say NO despite all their begging.

During the next week, to get more comfortable saying the word NO, consider picking an hour on the weekend to be "NO hour." Anything your kids ask, just say NO. Show them you can say NO. See how long it takes them to change the wording of the questions to have NO become the answer they want to hear. The important part comes when you are out shopping and you say NO and stick to your NO answer.

Consider watching the movie *Gremlins*. This movie does an excellent job of showing the importance of saying NO. The three rules that you need to obey when raising a Mogwai like Gizmo are: avoid bright light, don't get them wet, and never feed them after midnight. What happened if these rules were violated? Why was it important for Billy to say NO to the Mogwai? What precautions did Billy take to prevent breaking the rules? Have your kids think of other precautions Billy could have implemented.

Chapter 14
Play Board Games That Focus on Money

Encourage your children to play board games that involve handling money responsibly. I know this makes me sound old and outdated, but working with physical money is important. It needs to be tangible (Chapter 12). Nothing is better than hands-on experience.

Growing up, my friend Jodi and I loved to play board games like Life, Pay Day, and Monopoly. When playing Life, we wanted to avoid the poorhouse like the plague. Many times when we played Monopoly or Pay Day, the bank would go broke. In Monopoly, our games were long, because we played conservatively. We only bought property that we felt we could afford, mimicking that same prudence when we built houses and hotels. We looked ahead to see which properties we might land on and made sure we had enough money set aside for the rent via a large cash reserve. We also felt mortgaging property was to be avoided at all costs.

Jodi and I were rather risk-averse and played for the long run. There were few games that ended in one of us going bankrupt. Usually we just got tired of playing because the games never ended. As we played, we could fantasize what it would be like to have money. The games let us feel the difference between having enough money and not. When we had money the game was fun and easy. However, if the game was not working out in our favor and money was thin, the game was stressful, and rolling the dice became a dreaded chore. I believe playing games that involved money had a huge impact on our lives. We both respect money and made working with it the focus of our careers. Jodi has a master's degree in accountancy with a specialization in tax and is an executive tax director at a blue chip company.

Keep your money organized

Sadly, many people run their financial lives the same way they play Monopoly. When I play with other adults (yes, I still love to play), I am amazed at how aggressively some people play the game by buying property with their last dollar and having no back-up money for rent. Their safety net is to land on Free Parking to win the big pot of money in the middle, or to pass GO with the luck of the dice as their only plan. I have even seen some people enjoy being in jail since it delays the pain of going around the board with little money for rent.

Your MoneyBags Mission

Pick a day of the week to call game night and begin playing board games with your kids. Monopoly and Pay Day are excellent starter money games. Once your kids can handle the math well, consider introducing them to Life and the Monopoly Here & Now version. Both games will give them a more realistic view of life, where rent is in the thousands versus six dollars. They can also make choices about their income and insurance. Monopoly is a great way to teach bartering (Chapter 46), by trading properties to gain all of one color to create a monopoly. Avoid the Monopoly Electronic Banking edition, where the money is loaded to bank cards. Plain old play money needs to be in your children's hands.

Make the banker become the coveted role of the game. Start the game by selecting the banker; to keep things fair, choose by drawing straws, rolling the dice, or playing rock, paper, scissors. In Monopoly, if you have more than one child, repeat the process to determine who will be the property manager.

As your kids play, test their knowledge by allowing them to figure out how much they owe in rent. Avoid saying the color of the money ("You owe five pinks"), since real U.S. currency is not different colors. Simply tell them the amount and see how they do.

Teach your kids the importance of keeping their money organized versus in a scattered pile of cash. If you have a scattered pile of cash, you have no idea how much money you have. If you keep it organized and in stacks of bills from smallest denomination to largest, you have a better sense of your financial standing. One fun way to help your kids see the importance of organizing their money is to do a random "POP Money Count" a couple of times throughout the game. For example, if you see someone's money is in a huge pile, yell, "POP Money Count," and tell everyone to count their money. The first one done gets $50 from the bank and the last one done pays Free Parking or Jackpot $5. If the players' ages or skills are unbalanced, have an adult team up with the child that needs a little help, or give them a five-, ten-, or thirty-second head start.

Consider adopting the organization of money in your daily life, if you don't already. Have fun with how you handle and respect money by simply organizing it. Grab your purse or wallet and have your kids organize your money: all bills flattened out and facing one way with the presidents' heads all upright. Put the smallest bills first and follow with larger bills. Now, going forward, when you get cash back, you can make a big event of it. You can do Tim Conway's annoying routine as the white-haired old man character on *The Carol Burnett Show* from the 1970s . (Look it up on the Internet if you have no idea what I am talking about; it is worth your time to find him doing this act.) If you go into the slow old-man routine, telling your kids, "Wait . . . I got to get the Abe Lincolns behind the George Washingtons," and carefully arrange your money. You will make your kids crazy, especially if you do it at the cash register with a line behind you!

Recommended game tweaks:

Pay Day

Lottery: When your kids land on a lottery square, only allow one role of the die per person versus rolling until there is a winner. If no one wins, put the money back into the pot.

Monopoly Here & Now

Large denominations: It is likely your children will not understand the magnitude of the differences between $10,000, $100,000, and $1,000,000. One way to teach them fast is to start showing them the difference in Monopoly money. You can do this a couple of ways. In the beginning of the game, have your kids deal out the money to the different players. Make sure to encourage them to count out the dollar amounts (ten thousand, twenty thousand, etc.) versus five white, five pink, and six green. At the beginning of each game, until they understand, explain to them the difference in denominations: ten $10,000 bills equals one $100,000, and ten $100,000 bills equals one $1,000,000 bill.

If your kids experience some trouble, such as paying $100,000 when the rent is $10,000, show them the mistake by making a pile of money equaling the difference of $90,000. Usually, their eyes pop and their errors start going down. It is fun to see how fast they tend to catch on to the importance of the decimal place.

Life

Getting Married: When getting married, do an extra spin on the wheel for wedding costs. Simply spin the wheel and multiple the number it stops on by $2,000. For example, if you spin 8, then you pay $16,000 (8 x $2,000 = $16,000) to the bank.

A Child is Born: When a child is born, enjoy receiving your presents, but reduce your future salary by $1,000 for each child when you pass Pay Days to cover daycare and other expenses that come with having a baby.

Life Insurance: When you have the option to purchase life insurance, make sure to take a minute to explain life insurance to your kids. Basically, it protects the family from lost income if the person whose life is insured dies. For example, "If Dad is the breadwinner in the family and he dies, not only would the family be sad and miss him, but it means the family will no longer receive his paychecks. To protect the family, it is wise to purchase life insurance. Thus, in the event Dad dies, there will be a one-time payout of cash equal to the death benefit amount that was purchased."

In the game, create more realistic rules when someone lands on a life insurance death benefit space. The first time someone lands on a space that pays out a life insurance death benefit, it means that they lose the breadwinner, so they need to remove a peg from their car. If life insurance was purchased, collect the death benefit proceeds. Going forward, the spouse's new salary is reduced to 50% of the original breadwinner's salary. If life insurance was not purchased, the breadwinner is still removed and the spouse will still collect a salary that is 50% of the breadwinner's salary, but no life insurance proceeds will be paid.

After this first death, the player needs to decide if they would like to purchase a new life insurance policy on the surviving spouse by paying $10,000. Going forward, this will protect the reduced salary. Then, if a player lands on the life insurance payout space a second time, they collect the proceeds, if a new life insurance policy was purchased. Now the remaining spouse peg needs to be removed. If the player has no kids, the game is over. If the player has kids, the kids can proceed along the board, but going forward they will not receive a salary when landing or passing Pay Day since there is no breadwinner. Furthermore, the kids cannot buy another life insurance policy, since they do not have an insurable income (i.e., no one is bringing home a salary). If life insurance was not purchased to protect the spouse's income, the same rules above apply, but no death benefit will be paid.

Day of Reckoning: On the day of reckoning, don't collect $48,000 for each child, but rather pay $48,000 per child for college tuition.

Note: *For free game tweak printouts to store with your games, go to MoneyBagsLife.com.*

PART 2
MoneyBags Mindset
(Behavior and Skills)

Money Personalities and Perceptions

Chapter 15
Money Personality Spectrum

It is apparent that different people handle money differently. With a little thought, you can identify your own money personality, as well as the personalities of people around you. Think of it this way: if a person were to receive $1,000, what would be his or her tendency in handling the newfound money?

The most financially frugal and conservative personality type in handling money is the Hoarder. A Hoarder is the ultimate saver. They have mastered the concept of delayed gratification and live frugally, but they tend to miss the joy in spending money. Hoarders are fear-based. They are always worried that they

89

may run out of money, so security is important to them. They are not concerned about fitting in and are sometimes outcasts. So, without hesitation, they would save all of the money.

Savers are people who value and respect the freedom that money provides. These people save for their future, but also enjoy the fruits of today. They usually have good self-esteem, are disciplined, and are used to reaching goals that they set for themselves. They believe in hard work, but not working forever. They see the value of setting money aside now for future gain, whether it is education or investments. Like Hoarders, they tend to have a good hold on delayed gratification. In the case of $1,000, they would likely allocate up to half to paying down debt or buying something, and save the balance.

Nickel & Dimers are people with good intentions who tend to work hard to save money by using coupons. They have the mindset to save money, but they spend a little here and there with no real sense of where the money goes or anything to really show for it. To them, money is elusive. They want to save the $1,000, but they will spend most of it on the little things here and there on the way to the bank, such as five dollars for coffee, thirty dollars for a manicure, twenty dollars for a DVD, and so on.

Money Monks are people who continually give money away to people or charities. They feel it is a higher calling, or that they are not worthy compared to people in need. They trust in a higher power to always provide money when needed or a belief that everything will "work out." Money Monks will take the unexpected windfall of $1,000 and pay it forward to help someone.

Avoiders are people who find dealing with money painful. These people may have had no exposure to money growing up or possibly an unpleasant experience. They were likely raised to think money was too big or difficult to handle, so they avoid it at all costs. This avoidance becomes a self-fulfilling prophecy. Because they avoid money, the problems don't go away or fix themselves, but instead mushroom via late fees, penalties, or other consequences for not addressing money issues. Due  to the avoidance, they tend to have low self-esteem around money, even if they are confident in other parts of their life. In turn, this causes them to feel bad and want to avoid the issue more. They tend to be unable to say no to the money needs of others. Since they avoid conflict around money, they have a hard time staying disciplined or prioritizing their money needs. Often they don't budget, and they say "yes" when spending on other people. If they run out of money or need to cut corners to make ends meet, they choose to deprive themselves of needed items. In other words, they always pay themselves last. The Avoider would likely

How would you handle $1,000?

not take the needed steps to collect the $1,000 and it would go unclaimed.

Spenders tend to want to "fit in," and value how others perceive them. There is no surprise on what a Spender will do with an unexpected windfall of money—spend it, of course! They enjoy new shiny things and keeping up with the Joneses, and tend to jump to the Icing Level of the Money Hierarchy Cake. Spenders focus on the short-term (instant gratification) with little foresight on consequences, which can lead to low self-esteem. Their short-term spending can sabotage their long-term goals. There is a disconnect in peoples' perception of Spenders as having a lot of money, versus the reality that they have little to no savings and possibly large amounts of debt. Spenders may worry that their "secret" will be exposed and their house of cards will crumble. Spenders value the here and now and will worry about tomorrow later.

The most extreme money personality is the Taker. The Taker is focused on people giving them money versus making money. They can be mild, such as persistent mooches, or severe, such as pickpockets or the Bernie Madoffs of the world. Takers range from people who are always asking for money to people who swindle others out of money. Ironically, Takers sometimes work so hard at avoiding work that, in the end, if they had applied that much effort in traditional ways, they would have made a lot of their own money. A true Taker would not only take their $1,000, but also look for a way to get more.

Your MoneyBags Mission

For fun, have your kids draw pictures of the different personalities and what their "stuff," such as their houses and cars, might look like. As they are drawing, ask them the following questions. How do Hoarders act and feel about money? Does it give them joy? Does it give them anxiety? Does it provide them a feeling of safety? Does it scare them? Does it overwhelm them? Then, go to the next personality, asking the same questions.

As a family, think seriously about the different money personalities. Go through each one slowly with your kids and, without judgment, assess everyone's money personality. If someone has a personality that they don't like, tell them that this is their MoneyBags Moment. Consider going through Doug Lennick's Freeze game to retrain your brain's wiring. When you feel yourself acting in negative ways toward money, tell yourself to FREEZE. Then go through the four steps: Recognize, Reflect, Reframe, and Respond. First, recognize your instinctive behavior and natural response. Now, reflect: what are you feeling (anxious, stressed, overwhelmed)? Why do you feel this way? Were you told money was too complicated? Then, reframe. Rewire your brain. "I can handle this. It is just a bill that needs to be paid by the first of the month. No big deal, I will just quickly write a check and pay it now."

Going forward, choose what personality you want and strive to make the needed changes. You can begin by reprogramming your self-talk.

Chapter 16
The Myth that Rich People are Mean and Evil

When I was in college I had a roommate who LOVED the movie *It's a Wonderful Life*. I had never seen it and thought, *Why on earth does she like this old black-and-white movie?* Immediately, the movie goes into describing the characters, and I will never forget the introduction of Mr. Potter as "the richest, meanest man in the county." Well, I must admit, my friend was right; it is now my favorite movie. However, it is also a good example of how the entertainment industry has portrayed rich people as mean and evil. In the movies, rich people are often stereotyped as greedy, selfish, underhanded, conniving, and cheating, because that is the only way they can have more money than me, right? T. Harv Eker, author of *Secrets of the Millionaire Mind: Mastering the Inner Game of Wealth*, states that if you view rich people as mean and greedy, you will subconsciously not allow yourself to be rich, since you see rich people as having traits that you don't respect.

Your MoneyBags Mission

Have your kids think of five TV or movie characters, or real people, that are rich and mean. Then have them think of five really nice and respected rich people. Which were easier to name: the mean people or the nice people?

Over the next month as a family, watch these movies and discuss the main characters.

It's a Wonderful Life—George Bailey and Mr. Potter

$ Why is George considered rich?

$ If George had tons of money, do you think his personality would change?

$ How cool would it have been if George had been able to do his job and travel the world?

$ Why did helping people own houses versus renting them have such a positive impact on the people?

$ Why did home ownership have such a positive effect on the town?

$ Why did Mr. Potter want the Bailey Building & Loan to close?

$ If Mr. Potter had no money, would he be nice?

Pursuit of Happyness—Chris Gardner

$ What sacrifices, risks, and extra efforts did he make to go the extra mile and pursue his dream?

$ What obstacles did he have to overcome? Which one do you think was the most difficult?

$ If he had a lot of money today (which he does), would he be a nice guy or a mean guy?

After watching the movies, talk about the different characters. Were they mean people? Were they honest? Were they considerate of others in obtaining their money, or did they step on them? Did they, at all times, have the power within them to choose how they treated people? Is it possible that money has nothing to do with how people behave? In other words, if they are mean people, isn't it likely that they would be mean with or without money?

Ask your kids to imagine that they are really rich. Then ask them what nice things they would do with their money. How would they feel if people suddenly assumed that they were mean and greedy just because they had money?

To break your negative financial blueprint, consider reading T. Harv Eker's book. It explores your financial blueprint and how it affects your financial success, as well as the differences in the thinking of "rich" and "poor" people. Once you reach the "Wealth Files," walk your kids through one weekly.

Chapter 17
How Big is Their MoneyBag?

The movie *Pretty Woman*, starring Julia Roberts as Vivian, is a classic. Vivian is a professional escort whose customer turns out to be a rich business tycoon and the man of her dreams. The part I love is when Edward, played by Richard Gere, gives Vivian money so she can buy "respectable" clothes. She goes shopping on Rodeo Drive, the upscale boutique district in Beverly Hills. She is excited to spend Edward's money, but no one will wait on her because she does not "look" like she has money. Later in the film, when Edward finds out that her shopping spree was sabotaged, he cancels all of his appointments for the day to go shopping with her. He enters a store with the air of someone dripping of money. He tells the salespeople that he is going to spend an obscene amount of money. After a couple of hours of shopping and thousands of dollars spent, Edward returns to work. Vivian, however, backtracks to the store where the shopkeepers refused to wait on her. She enters and says, "Do you remember me? You work on commission right?" She then lifts up all of her shopping bags in her hands, looks at them, flashes her huge smile, and laughs, "Big mistake, big, HUGE!"

As a family of entrepreneurs in a rural area, we had a couple of sayings. "If they have mud on their shoes then they have money in their pockets" and "Don't assume that how someone dresses determines if they are poor." In other words, don't judge the bag lady until you see what is in her bag.

So how do you know if someone is "rich"? I find this to be an interesting question. As an outsider, it is hard to determine who is prudent with their money. Most people do it the only way they can—by calculating the amount of "nice stuff" people own. This, however, is not a good measure since people who have all the "toys" don't always have money set aside in investments. In other words, many times people think the Spenders are the ones with all the money because of their "stuff." A Spender will be open to buying a new car every couple of years, while Savers and Hoarders tend to drive their cars "into the ground" before purchasing their next cars. Savers and Hoarders see cars as a poor investment since they depreciate, losing their value over time. The car simply exists to get them from point A to point B. Don't get me wrong, many rich people buy nice cars, but they don't pay for extremely expensive things until they reach the Icing Level and can afford to splurge. Rich people limit their debt and save money on a regular basis to invest in appreciating assets, such as stocks, bonds, or mutual funds, that tend to grow in value over time.

As a Certified Financial Planner I get to see everything in a client's financial house. I know their income, goals, and money personality. I also know if they are working toward their goals by being disciplined or if they are jumping to the Icing Level. Lastly, I know my clients' net worth, which is an excellent measure of financial success. To calculate your net worth, simply add up all of your assets (stuff you own) and subtract all of your liabilities (money you owe).

What is your target net worth?

The book *The Millionaire Next Door* by Thomas J. Stanley, Ph.D., and William D. Danko Ph.D., does an excellent job of describing typical millionaires. As stated above, too many people assume the amount of one's depreciating assets (cars, boats, watches, clothes, etc.) is a good measure of one's wealth. In reality, your typical millionaire is investing money in appreciating assets and spending little on depreciating assets. In the book, the authors discuss a rule of thumb to determine if your net worth is strong relative to your income: Take your age multiplied by your gross income and then divide by ten. For example, if your income is $50,000 and you are 30 years old, then your target net worth is $150,000 ($50,000 x 30

= $1,500,000 and $1,500,000 / 10 = $150,000). If your net worth is equal to or greater than your target, you are doing great, if it is below, you need to look at what you can do differently to improve your net worth going forward.

> **Note:** *People often overestimate the resale value of depreciating assets. For example, if they paid $35,000 for a car, people assume that they can sell it for $30,000-$35,000 five years later, when actually the value may have dropped in half to $15,000. The reality is that once you drive the car off the lot, the value goes down substantially and continues to drop as the car gets older, damaged by everyday wear and tear. Thus, be conservative in your estimates.*

Your MoneyBags Mission

Calculate your target net worth. As a good personal exercise, calculate and track your net worth quarterly. To calculate, take your assets (house, cars, cash, investments, retirement plans) less liabilities (mortgage, home equity loan, car loans, credit card debt, student loans). For a free and easy net worth worksheet, go to MoneyBagsLife.com.

Consider getting your kids in the habit of tracking their net worths quarterly. As your children cross milestones ($10, $100, $1,000 and so on) make sure to congratulate them and acknowledge their hard work and discipline.

When you are out and about people-watching or driving down the road, randomly have fun trying to guess whether someone is "rich." How did you draw this conclusion? Do you think maybe that person spends every dollar they make and has no money saved? How about when you see a small house—is the owner poor? Is it possible they have spent little money and have saved or invested most of what they earn?

Consider reading *The Millionaire Next Door.* This book does an excellent job of explaining the statistical facts about "millionaires." If you are not a big reader, step out of your comfort zone. Consider making it a family project to read a section weekly with your kids as part of your commitment to exposing your kids to good money management.

Behaviors of Good Money Managers

Chapter 18
All Actions Have Consequences

My favorite law is Sir Isaac Newton's third law of motion: For every action there is an equal and opposite reaction. Teach your kids about consequences. Although consequences have a negative connotation, they can be good or bad. For example, if your children maintain good grades and go to college, they will experience positive consequences for their good behavior.

My parents always taught me that there are consequences for my actions and that they would not interfere with me experiencing those consequences. Conversely, I am sure you know some parents who will do anything to avoid having their kids experience negative consequences, whether it is a poor grade, serving a detention, or not completing their homework.

In my family, we have stories of how prior generations experienced consequences. It kept the rest of us on the straight and narrow—no need to tempt fate. One legendary story in my family is about my Uncle Ross. He was attending college at the University of Illinois and traveled home for a short holiday. However, once he was home, he decided he was not going to return to school. Surprisingly, my great-grandfather said, "No problem." The next day, my great grandfather woke up his son at the crack of dawn and told him that if he was not going to go to school, then he WAS going to work. He gave him a manual post-hole-digging tool and told him to build a fence. Needless to say, Ross was not a manual labor kind of guy, and he caught the next train back to school.

How this story relates to money is twofold. First, I am sure my great-grandfather did not enjoy footing the bill for Ross's college education and then seeing that money thrown out the window. Second, Ross got a glimpse of what his life might be like without a degree by feeling the consequences. This defining moment propelled his life forward. Once he graduated from college, his career led him to be a part-owner and major shareholder of the local bank; he became Johnson County State's Attorney, was elected First Judicial Circuit Judge from 1945 to1970, and was appointed Third District Appellate Judge by the Illinois Supreme Court.

Your MoneyBags Mission

A fun childhood game that does an excellent job of teaching kids about consequences is Truth or Dare. I remember as a little kid that the dare was the wild card I did not enjoy. For me, telling the truth was the conservative choice. As a family, play a friendly game of Truth or Dare. Allow your kids to pick their poison and experience the consequences of the path they take.

For the next week, focus on helping your kids see the pros and cons of their decisions and let them experience consequences for better or worse. For example, if they don't want to do their homework, explain that they will have consequences for their decisions. It can be the punishment that you have decided to deliver (and make sure you follow through) for their poor decision and/or it is the low grade that will affect them down the road when they want to go to college. What if they kick the ball around in the house? What if they lose their allowance money for not completing their baseline chores? They fought you about going to bed? What if they were good little helpers in the kitchen or around the house? In all scenarios, it is their choice.

As a family, consider watching the movie *The Ultimate Gift*. Once you are through the first part of the movie, where Jason leaves the office after the will is read, stop the movie. Have everyone write on individual pieces of paper what they think is the ultimate gift and keep it secret. After the movie, open the pieces of paper and see who was the closest to the answer.

Ask your kids what their favorite scene in the movie was and why. Did a part of the movie seem identical to what happened to my Uncle Ross? What were the consequences that Jason experienced? Did those consequences cause him to rethink his behavior?

Chapter 19
Live within Your Means

"When a man sits with a pretty girl for an hour, it seems like a minute. But let him sit on a hot stove for a minute—then it's longer than any hour. That's relativity!"

—Albert Einstein

In a nutshell, the above quote means everything is relative—money, fun, whatever, is all measured on a scale. To live within your means has a different relativity for everyone. For example, spending $5,000 on an annual vacation may seem too expensive to some people, but can seem in line or even small to other people. This relativity is based on your circumstance. If you have a large income and few major expenses, $5,000 may not seem like a large dollar amount to spend on leisure.

However, if you have a modest income and four kids, this can seem like an impossible dream.

I never had much debt until I purchased my first home. I knew that buying a house versus renting was a good practice for the mere reason that at some point down the road (thirty years) I would no longer have a house payment. Moreover, the house would likely increase in value over time. Plus, if I continued renting not only would I always have a monthly rent payment, but due to the cost of living, the amount would likely increase over time. When I bought my house, the debt amount seemed HUGE. Now, looking back, I see it was a lot of debt "relative" to my situation, but not in comparison to other people's debt.

I have some clients who have modest incomes, with one parent at home raising their kids, and they are doing it all. They are saving for their financial and personal goals, while living within their means. I have other clients who make excellent incomes and struggle to build cash reserves, eliminate credit card debt, thinly fund their retirement plans, and continually pull equity out of their houses. It is important to have the mindset that, no matter what your income status is, you will find a way to live within your means. To do so, you have three choices: reduce your expenses (stop spending and lower your cash outlay), increase your income (change careers or get a second job), or a combination of the two. Sometimes you have to choose to increase your expenses in the short term, such as going back to school, to increase your income in the long term.

Be aware that it is natural to grow into your income. If your income is $50,000, and then you get a job that pays $100,000, your lifestyle tends to shift upward, reaching toward the Icing Level. Increasing your income is not an automatic fix to your financial problems. You have to make conscious decisions to be disciplined with good money management habits, such as paying down debt, limiting spending, and earmarking money toward savings.

Your MoneyBags Mission

Have your kids go around the house, randomly pick up five items each, and place them on the kitchen table.

Ask these questions.

$ Which one do you think is most expensive?

$ What can you think of that is more expensive than that?

$ Which one weighs the least?

$ What can you think of that is lighter than that?

$ Which one is the heaviest?

$ Can you think of things that are heavier than that?

MoneyBags Mindset (Behavior and Skills)

The Dr. Seuss movie and book *Horton Hears a Who!* does an excellent job of illustrating relativity. For fun, watch the movie or read the book. Ask your kids how they think the Whos felt when they found out how small they were. Is it possible that we are Whos, too? What if a Horton is carrying *us* around on a small flower?

Chapter 20
Budgeting

I vividly remember my father sitting me down in our backyard patio to discuss my budget before I left for college. He told me that I would receive a monthly allowance. He then went into detail about how much I would receive, what that money was to be spent on, and how I was to live within my budget. He factored in my rent, utilities, telephone, food, gas, insurance, fun money, and so on. He made it very clear to me that the amount allotted would be enough to meet my needs, and I was expected to live within those parameters. Like all good dads, he told me to call him if I really got into a bind, but that it should not be a monthly occurrence. Those clear parameters taught me a valuable lesson: live within my means. I never wanted to make that call home to ask for more money. I remember feeling trusted and empowered by that conversation, since I knew I had begun to cross over to adulthood. Meeting

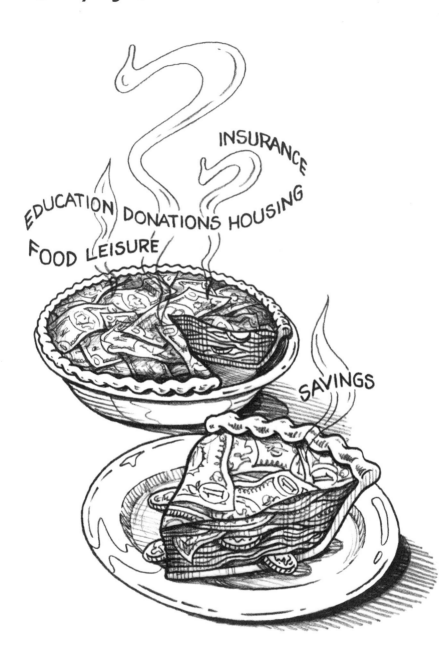

my parents' expectations via the challenge of living within my means gave me confidence and a sense of accomplishment, control, and pride.

In working with my clients over the years, I have found that nothing makes them squirm more than asking them to complete a budget. This is because a budget is the ultimate in accountability. Basically, in a budget, you list how much money you earn, and then begin subtracting: savings, taxes, and living expenses. Ideally, you are able to account for every penny. In other words, when you subtract your expenses, including savings, from your income, it should equal zero.

However, it is unrealistic to track your money that closely. Therefore, once you complete the budget, look at your final number. A positive number reflects a couple of outcomes: either you have a surplus, which is good and means you have discretionary income and are living within your means, or you have understated your expenses. If you are running up debt or having trouble covering your monthly expenses, you need to revisit and adjust your budget.

A negative final number can also reflect a couple of outcomes. If you have a problem in covering your obligations and are running into a deficit each month, then you are living outside of your means. Another reason you may have a negative number is that you easily meet all of your obligations, but you overstated your expenses in the budget.

If you are self-employed or on a commission income, budgeting is still important, but more challenging since you don't know how much you will earn or when the money will arrive. As a result, try to estimate what you feel is a low or safe estimate of your annual income, then budget for that amount. Throughout the year, it is important to set money aside to offset the lean months.

A budget helps to determine when you can and cannot spend your money. For example, if you need a new car and your discretionary income shows you can only afford a monthly payment of $250 without going over your budget, then you know how much you can spend on a car payment. So, if a car payment is $350, it takes your discretionary income to a negative, by $100. Thus, you must eliminate $100 that you spend elsewhere.

The same is true for your kids. If your children receive a $15 weekly allowance, which gives them $6 to spend ($15 x .40 = $6, according to the formula in Chapter 10), but they want a movie and candy every weekend, then they have to make sure they have enough money. If the movie costs $5 and candy is $2, can they afford their desired lifestyle? Do they have enough money, or would they run a deficit, spending money they do not have by borrowing money from you or siblings to get what they want? As parents, giving your children $1 or $2 here and there teaches them to live outside their means, and that lack of discipline could lead to future credit card debt.

Your MoneyBags Mission

As a family, figure out where you spend your money. Go to MoneyBagsLife.com to download a free budget form, or simply complete your budget on a sheet of paper. Do this by listing your income, money coming in the door, less your expenses, money going out the door (savings, taxes, charitable giving, and living expenses). If you have money left over at the end of the month, that is awesome! However, if you have a shortage (negative amount), you need to reduce your expenses or find a way to increase your income. As you adjust your options, remember that lowering your savings or taxes to make your budget work is a poor strategy. Once you know the amount of your monthly expenses, take it a step further and figure out the yearly amount, then break it down to the amount per day.

> **Note:** *If you are not ready for your kids to know all your detailed financial information, go through the above exercise by yourself. For the pie exercise below, assume your income is $1,000 a month, but use your actual percentages of various expenses.*

An excellent way to teach your kids about budgeting and living within their means is to have them divide up a pie. The beauty of a pie is that it illustrates living within your means. You have to adjust to the size of the pie (income). Explain to your kids that the pie is the size of the family income and you have to slice a sliver of pie for all your expenses. For example, tell your kids that the first slice they cut needs to be large enough for your savings—do it in proportion to the budget you created. Then slice a piece large enough to cover the percentage of taxes you owe and another piece large enough to cover your charitable giving. Continue to cut pieces in proportion to the percentages of your committed expenses (mortgage/rent, insurance, food, car loans, utility bills, and so on). Once your committed expenses are dished out, explain that the rest of the pie is to cover your discretionary expenses (hobbies, entertainment, dinning out, travel, clothing, and such). If you don't have enough pie to cover all your expenses, then you need to discuss options on how to fix the problem, such as getting a bigger pie (more income) or reducing the size of the expenses. Once you complete the exercise, enjoy eating the pie, so you don't waste money!

Let your kids learn about budgeting by allowing them to run the family money on weekends. On Saturday morning, tell your kids how much money they have to spend for the weekend. Then talk about your weekend plans. If they want to go to the zoo and then to the movies, let them know how much that will cost. Remind them that you need to go grocery shopping and run some errands for the house. If they are not careful it might turn into a day of all entertainment and no food. It is up to you to coach them on the importance of staying within a budget and meeting all goals. To increase your child's exposure to money, consider giving them the responsibility of holding the cash, depending on the amount of money and age of your children. At the very least, you hold the money, but let them pay the cashier.

If you have younger kids and the entire weekend budget is too complicated for them, you can put them in charge of a weekend meal. Give them a budget of $15 and have them pick out what they want for dinner. Then go to the store and buy the needed ingredients. If their total is over $15, make adjustments, such as they have to pick less expensive brands or forgo some ingredients. To incent them to be frugal, place the remaining change into the Family Savings Jar.

Chapter 21
Awareness of Ongoing Costs

Ongoing costs can be expensive. Living in Minnesota, the Land of 10,000 Lakes, I hear a common story from some of my clients that always makes me shake my head. It goes kind of like this.

> *Wendy: "So what is new and exciting since I last saw you?"*

> *Clients: "Well we bought a new boat and trailer."*

> *Wendy [thinking to herself]: So you increased your debt or spent down your assets. Plus, your expenses will go up since you need to insure the boat, buy a sufficient number of life vests, pay a slip fee and storage costs. Not to mention gas, which is always more expensive on water than on land.*

Wendy: "Do you have any other expenses you need to brace for in the next six months to a year?"

Clients: "We need to buy a truck since our current car cannot pull the boat."

Wendy [thinking to herself]: They will incur more debt or deplete more assets. Trucks usually cost more money than cars, plus they will want the four-wheel drive with the tow package, not to mention gas mileage will go down so their gas budget will go up.

At the end of the day, most people spend much more on their boat than they had planned due to ongoing costs. This reminds me of the book written by Rose Bonne, *I Know An Old Lady*. The book explains that the old lady swallows a fly. Then she swallows a spider to eat the fly. She proceeds to swallow a bird to catch the spider, a cat to catch the bird, a dog to catch the cat, a cow to catch the dog, and finally a horse—which is the death of her—of course!

Your MoneyBags Mission

Walk your kids through a couple of examples of ongoing costs of things. One that will likely hit home for them is the purchase of a pet. Determine the cost of owning and caring for a pet.

Example 1:

Let's say your kids want a puppy. Walk them through ALL the costs involved in dog ownership.

- **$** First you have to find the puppy. Sometimes this is inexpensive if you adopt from an animal shelter, but it can get costly if you purchase a dog from a breeder. Costs vary all over the country, so to keep it simple, let's assume you spend $100.

- **$** Now that you have the puppy home, what is next? Well, you need to purchase supplies for the puppy: food, bowls, pet bed, grooming products, toys, and leash, for starters. Let's say you spend $250 at the pet store.

- **$** It is recommended that you have your puppy seen by a veterinarian in the first week to make sure the dog is healthy and has all of its shots. Assume $100. Down the road it is a good idea to spay or neuter your dog if it was not done before the adoption, so let's assume it costs $100.

$ In the first several weeks, you need to housetrain the puppy and teach it not to chew on things. Over the course of the next month, it's fair to assume you will spend $100 on supplies and replacing destroyed items (obviously I am not counting that couch that got chewed up when you got home late one night).

$ Your pet is also more enjoyable if it is disciplined and knows commands, so let's assume you take your dog to obedience school: $150.

$ Now that you have had the dog for a month, how much has it cost you so far? ($100 + $250 + $100 + $100 + $100 +$150 = $800)

$ Your upfront investments are behind you, but what about ongoing costs? Your dog needs food, $50 per month, and annual trips to the vet: estimate $150. So far, it is at least $750 ($50 x 12 = $600, $600+ $150 = $750) each year.

$ So with the numbers given above, have your kids calculate how much the dog might cost you in the first year ($50 x 12 = $600, $600 + $150 = 750, $750 + $800 = $1,550).

$ If your dog lives for twelve years, what is the minimum cost over your dog's lifetime? ($750 x 12 = $9,000, $9,000 + $800 = $9,800)

💲 What things could increase the cost of owning a dog? For example, erecting a fence in your backyard, teeth cleaning and dental care as the dog ages. What if your dog gets sick or injured? Will you need to pay someone to take care of your dog if you go on vacation? How much does that cost? If you need to adjust your budget, what things could you cut back on? Remember, reducing your savings or taxes to offset the cost of a dog is not a good strategy.

Example 2:

Now have your kids calculate the cost of driving a HUGE truck (23 gallons per tank with an estimated gas mileage of 16 miles per gallon) versus a small car (13 gallons per tank with an estimated gas mileage of 28 miles per gallon).

💲 Have your kids calculate how much it will cost to fill up both cars if gas is $3 per gallon. (HUGE truck 23 x $3 = $69, and small car 13 x $3 = $39)

💲 How much will it cost if gas goes up to $5 per gallon? (HUGE truck 23 x $5 = $115 and small car 13 x $5 = $65)

$ Ask your kids to figure out how many miles they can travel on one tank of gas in the HUGE truck with a full tank of gas (23 x 16 = 368). How many miles can they travel in the small car on one full tank of gas? (13 x 28 = 364)

$ Have your kids calculate how much would it cost if you were going to drive 1,000 miles. Assume you need to fill up each automobile three times at $3 per gallon (HUGE truck $69 x 3 = $207 and small car $39 x 3 = $117). What if gas increases to $5 per gallon? (HUGE truck $115 x 3 = $345 and small car $65 x 3 = $195)

$ How much would it cost to fuel each car for a year? Assume you needed a tank of gas per week at $3 per gallon (HUGE truck $69 x 52 = $3,588 and small car $39 x 52 = $2,028). What is the cost at $5 per gallon? (HUGE truck $115 x 52 = $5,980 and small car $65 x 52 = $3,380)

$ If your monthly budget for gas is $140 and you need to fill up your car two times a month, at what price per gallon do you go over your budget? At $3 per gallon, both the HUGE truck and small car are within your budget (HUGE truck $69 x 2 = $138 and small car $39 x 2 = $78). However, at $5 per gallon, only the small car remains within the family budget (HUGE truck $115 x 2 = $230 and small car $65 x 2 = $130). If you drove the HUGE truck, you would be forced to lower your expenses by $90 a month to handle the increase in gas to $5 a gallon ($115 x 2 = $230, $230 - $140 = $90).

$ As a family, if you owned the HUGE truck and gas increased to $5 per gallon, what expenses would you choose to lower by $90 to live within your means? Fewer meals out or less entertainment? Remember, lowering savings or taxes is not a good option.

$ What things could lower your fuel bill, besides the price of gas decreasing? In the future, you could buy a car with better gas mileage (what if your car could go 75 miles on a gallon of gas?), or purchase a car that runs on alternative fuel, such as electricity. Things that you can do immediately include reducing the number of miles you drive by reducing errand runs, riding a bike, walking, or carpooling.

Chapter 22
Optimism

Ronald Reagan had a favorite joke about optimism.

The joke concerns twin boys of five or six. Worried that the boys had developed extreme personalities—one was a total pessimist, the other a total optimist—their parents took them to a psychiatrist.

First the psychiatrist treated the pessimist. Trying to brighten his outlook, the psychiatrist took him to a room piled to the ceiling with brand-new toys. But instead of yelping with delight, the little boy burst into tears. "What's the matter?" The psychiatrist asked, baffled. "Don't you want to play with any of the toys?"

"Yes," the little boy bawled, "but if I did, I'd only break them."

> *Next the psychiatrist treated the optimist.*
> *Trying to dampen his outlook, the psychiatrist*
> *took him to a room piled to the ceiling with*
> *horse manure. But instead of wrinkling his nose*
> *in disgust, the optimist emitted just the yelp of*
> *delight that the psychiatrist had been hoping*
> *to hear from his brother, the pessimist. Then he*
> *clambered to the top of the pile, dropped to his*
> *knees, and began gleefully digging out scoop*
> *after scoop with his bare hands. "What do you*
> *think you are doing?" the psychiatrist asked, just*
> *as baffled by the optimist as he had been by the*
> *pessimist.*
> *"With all this manure," the little boy*
> *replied, beaming, "there must be a pony in here*
> *somewhere!"* [2]

Teach your kids to be optimistic. I know this may seem strange in a book about money, but if your children are scared to take risks in life or lose money, it reduces their self-confidence and investment options down the road. Furthermore, to be successful in almost any profession, it helps if you can see the bright side of all situations. For example, in a down market when stock prices are low, people lose money. However, the people who are optimistic that the market will rebound realize that this is a huge opportunity to buy or hold,

---

[2]   http://gregghake.com/2010/02/the-pony-in-the-dung-heap-ron-ald-reagan-eleanor-roosevelt-and-you/

since historically the stock market will go back up. The optimists are the ones who make lots of money, which involves calculated risk.

Your MoneyBags Mission

A fun exercise that I learned from one of T. Harv Eker's programs is to "feel" the difference of optimism and pessimism by acting. Have everyone in the family walk around the house being pessimistic about EVERYTHING, from the carpet being the wrong color, to the food tasting bland, to your pets being bored. Walk around the house as grumpy as possible for five minutes. Then, do the reverse. For the next five minutes, be optimistic and positive about EVERYTHING, like how beautiful the rain is, and how it feeds the plants and makes fun puddles to jump in. Continue on about the way you love the thirty stairs you have to climb multiple times a day, which provides you awesome exercise, and so on.

After five minutes, gather up your kids and ask them what they felt. Did they enjoy feeling grumpy over happy? Did their energy levels change? Did they notice that they just needed to flip a mental switch to change their attitudes?

If you have a child who is constantly saying negative things, consider doing what a friend of mine did— catch your child making a negative statement and challenge them to say five positive things before they say another negative. She came up with this strategy when she drove her son and a pessimistic boy to school a couple of times a week. The boy was so negative, it was driving her crazy. He went on and on about how he hated school, the weather, cafeteria food, the teachers, and so on. She got so fed up with his negative attitude that she refused to start the car until both boys told her five positive things about their day before they could say one negative thing. Initially, the boy had a difficult time thinking of good things to say, but after a week he hardly ever mentioned negative things.

You can make this part of your daily ritual by having your kids name five things that they are grateful for at the dinner table, before going to bed, or before you start the car.

For the next month, focus on being optimistic as a family. Every day, if something is perceived as bad or negative, find a way to look on the bright side. For example, what if a fire in your house destroyed your clothes? Try to find some pros in this situation, like thanks to your homeowners insurance, you get to buy some new clothes. You get the idea. Now practice, what would be the pros ... if you had a fender bender with your brand new car? If someone spilled a drink on you? If you missed an important test at school due to illness?

Chapter 23
Be Contrary

If you asked my best friend from my hometown to describe me, his first word would be *contrary*. To me, the definition of contrary is doing the exact opposite of what is expected, avoiding a "follow the herd" mentality. To me, following the herd seems too easy and unoriginal. In high school, a group of my girlfriends loved to dress like Madonna and I thought, what is the point? *Why follow a look someone else created?*

In part, I learned to avoid being part of the herd from Imogene. From her name alone, you can tell she was one of a kind and followed the beat of a different drummer. One of the ways she entertained my sister and me was with a game she created, which I call Russian Roulette driving. The game was quite simple. In Vienna, there are lots of four-way stops. When she came to an intersection, she would have us guess which way she was going to go. If we told her right, she would fake a right and then safely do a hard left that whipped my sister and me around in our seats. This happened turn after turn. We would say one way and she would go the other, making us all laugh hysterically.

The reason I bring this up is that one way to teach your kids to be financially savvy is to teach them early to avoid blindly following the herd. One classic movie

Challenge the thinking of the masses

scene that demonstrates the silliness of herd mentality is the homecoming parade scene in *Animal House.* Due to sabotage by the Deltas, the marching band takes a right turn and follows the drum major down a dead end. Being good followers, they keep marching forward, with everyone bumping each other and smashing up against a brick wall. Ironically, I experienced this with a gaggle of financial advisors. We traveled as a group to New York City, deplaned, and started following the herd. Sure enough, we had been walking for several minutes, covering a great distance in the airport, when suddenly there was a halt and great confusion. Apparently, the "leader" did not know where we were supposed to go; he was just the first one off the airplane. As unbelievable as it may seem, we were all blindly following along. No one asked any questions; we just assumed that we were following the person in charge.

Avoiding the herd mentality requires you to stop and challenge the thinking of the masses. On that same New York trip, our group of advisors visited several financial institutions to hear different mutual fund managers talk and explain their investment styles. The strategies varied a bit, but they all told us they were "contrary." So, if everyone is contrary, are you contrary? On that trip I had the honor of listening to one of my favorite mutual fund managers speak about his investment style and logic. His approach was totally different, and he was the only one who convinced me he was contrary. After 9/11, he bought airline stock when everyone else was selling. After Hurricane Katrina, he invested in property and casualty insurance companies. During the down market of 2008, he purchased recreational and leisure stocks. When these events occurred, the masses were moving one way (selling) and he was moving the opposite way (buying). These were all excellent long-term decisions. He was able to pick up the stocks dirt cheap, hold them, and wait for them to turn around once the masses felt it was safe to buy again—which then drove the prices back up.

Your MoneyBags Mission

In the movie *Dead Poets Society*, starring Robin Williams, my favorite scene is when Robin's character is in the courtyard with his class, and he tells them to walk "their" unique walk. The boys begin creating different ways to walk by limping, skipping, and going backward, but one guy just stands there. Robin asks the student why he isn't walking, and the boy responds that he is "exercising the right not to walk."

For fun, mimic the *Dead Poets Society* and have the whole family create a unique walk. Go a step further and have everyone in the family create their own unique MoneyBags nickname. When you and your kids are talking about money, use everyone's MoneyBags names! For example, I have a group of bowling friends. Everyone has a unique and fun bowling name. They call me "Money" and I love it!

Chapter 24
The Power of Doubling

There's a famous legend about the origin of chess:

When the inventor of the game showed it to the emperor of India, the emperor was so impressed by the new game, he said to the man "Name your reward!"

The man responded, "Oh emperor, my wishes are simple. I only wish for this. Give me one grain of rice for the first square of the chessboard, two grains for the next square, four for the next, eight for the next and so on for all sixty-four squares, with each square having double the number of grains as the square before."

The emperor agreed, amazed that the man had asked for such a small reward—or so he thought. After a week, his treasurer came back and informed him that the reward would add up to an astronomical sum, far greater than all the rice that could conceivably be produced in many many centuries." [3]

People often wonder how fast their money will grow. Due to many variables and no crystal ball, assumptions and rules of thumb are handy tools. One way to determine how fast your money will double with compounding interest (see Chapter 51) is the Rule of 72. On a high level, if you want to know when your $1,000 investment will become $2,000, you can divide the interest rate into 72 for the answer. For example, if you assume an 8% interest rate, it will take 9 years (72 / 8 = 9) for your $1,000 to turn into $2,000. Pretty cool!

Your MoneyBags Mission

Have your kids practice the Rule of 72. For example, assume they have $1 million dollars, invested at 6%. How long until they have $2 million? (72 / 6 = 12 years.) What if they got a 7% interest rate? (72 / 7 = 10.285 years.)

So they can visually see the power of doubling, consider this little game to bring the point home. To get started, give your kids 100 pennies (or a small bag of rice) and a chessboard.

As in the story, have your kids place a penny on a square. Tomorrow, have them double it and place two

3.   http://www.dr-mikes-math-games-for-kids.com/rice-and-chess-board.html

pennies on another square, the next day four pennies, and so on. As you can see from the chart below, the growth of pennies doubling daily is amazing!

Ask them how long until they run out of pennies. How far do they get before they see the compounding? At the end of the month, how much will they have set aside? How far did they go before they had to give up (i.e., when did the 100 pennies run out)? Did they want to jump into their piggy banks or use their allowance money to keep the game going? How did they feel when they could not double their money?

1st	$0.01	17th	$655.36
2nd	$0.02	18th	$1,310.72
3rd	$0.04	19th	$2,621.44
4th	$0.08	20th	$5,242.88
5th	$0.16	21st	$10,485.76
6th	$0.32	22nd	$20,971.52
7th	$0.64	23rd	$41,943.04
8th	$1.82	24th	$83,886.08
9th	$2.56	25th	$167,772.16
10th	$5.12	26th	$335,544.32
11th	$10.24	27th	$671,088.64
12th	$20.48	28th	$1,342,177.28
13th	$40.96	29th	$2,684,354.56
14th	$81.92	30th	$5,368,709.12
15th	$163.84	31st	$10,737,418.24
16th	$327.68		

Chapter 25
The Importance of Delayed Gratification

Teach your children the fun of delayed gratification versus impulse buying. Delayed gratification is the feeling you experience when you avoid short-term temptations as a tradeoff for a larger reward later, such as when you save money for a trip, car, house, or retirement. Conversely, impulse buying is a random, spontaneous purchase. It is when you buy things you don't need simply because they appear to be fun at the moment. You had not planned on buying these things; they just happened to be there, like in the checkout aisle at grocery stores. Impulse buying is when you buy out of the feeling of wanting this new and shiny thing that is often outside your budget and goals. As you are aware, we are all wired for instant gratification. Technology has brought us microwaves, cell phones, text messaging, email, not to mention advances in other areas such as medical science.

A fascinating longitudinal study completed in the 1960s demonstrates the power of delayed gratification as well as some startling advantages. A researcher named Walter Mischel put a marshmallow on a plate in front of four-year-old children and gave them instructions. They were allowed to eat the marshmallow, but if the child was willing to wait to eat the treat when he came back from a short break, they would receive a second marshmallow. Once alone, the kids were observed, one at a time, to see if they would give into temptation and eat the marshmallow.

Some children waited the entire ten or fifteen minutes he was gone and earned the second marshmallow (waiters), while others ate the marshmallow the second he left the room (grabbers). However, the more important findings came from following up on the children in the study. The study actually "demonstrated that the amount of time a child could wait was an almost direct predictor of future academic and personal success. Fourteen years later, Mischel found that the 'grabbers' suffered low self-esteem and were viewed by others as stubborn, prone to envy, and easily frustrated. The 'waiters' had better coping skills, were more socially competent, self-assertive, trustworthy, dependable, academically successful, and scored about 210 points higher on the SATs. In fact, the ability to delay gratification through self-discipline (as measured by the

'Marshmallow Test') was a better predictor of future success than any other measurement."[4]

A classic example of teaching delayed gratification in my family revolved around my favorite holiday, Christmas. Like all kids, my sister and I loved Santa Claus. My parents used this holiday (and Santa) to the fullest. The months before Christmas were further intensified since my dad owned a retail store. My sister and I worked the weekends, wrapping packages, so we saw the hustle and bustle of the mall build up to the magical day.

Delayed gratification is directly tied to your child's success

In the months before Christmas, if we wanted anything, my parents would tell us to ask Santa for it at Christmas. If we were behaving poorly, they reminded us of his naughty list and that we would only get a lump of coal. We would look through magazines, dreaming about what we wanted, and we wrote letters to the North Pole listing our wishes to Santa.

To add more excitement, my mom loves to decorate for the holidays. At our house, the flip from Thanksgiving to Christmas just added fuel to the fire, which was further amplified as the pile of magnificently wrapped presents grew quietly under the tree. To add to the

---

4.   http://www.princetonacademy.org/weblogs/heads-journal/ archives/Images/Microsoft%20Word%20-%20Olen's%20letter. pdf (accessed July 2011).

suspense, my mom always bought an Advent calendar, which allowed us to count the days and find a surprise behind each panel.

Unlike many kids, we were not allowed to open presents on Christmas Eve, though my sister and I tried to sway my parents. Trying to sleep that night was impossible. My sister and I would sneak into the family room in the wee hours of the morning to see if Santa ate the cookies and drank the milk we left him by the fireplace. Once we saw the cookies were gone, we would check out the presents he brought us, wrapped with special paper, placed under the tree, and bursting from our stockings! Oh, the joy! Filled with excitement, we had to wait until 6:00 a.m. before my parents would finally give in and let us open our presents (the one day a year that we would drag them out of bed versus them getting us out of bed).

For most families, once the presents were opened and played with, the day was over, but not in my family. My mother is an excellent cook, so MoneyBags and Imogene always joined us for the holiday family meal. Throughout the day we waited for them to arrive to have our second Christmas gift exchange. The fireplace made our house cozy, holiday music played, the dinner table was formally set, and the house smelled delicious from the big meal being prepared. Once we were all together, we opened our second round of presents, ate our dinner, and topped off the evening with the homemade cookies that my mom made for the season. Oh, the joy of delayed gratification!

Your MoneyBags Mission

For fun, test your kids on delayed gratification, just as Walter Mischel did, by putting them in a room with a marshmallow (or favorite treat) on a plate and saying, "I have to leave the room for fifteen minutes. If you don't eat this marshmallow before I return, I will give you another one." Then, leave the room for fifteen minutes. When you return, if the marshmallow is still there, your child is doing an excellent job of delaying gratification! Compliment your child and give them the promised reward. However, if you come back and that marshmallow is half eaten or gone, you need to really work on building the rewards for delayed gratification.

Note: *If you are good with technology consider hiding a video or web camera to watch how your kids handle their time alone with the marshmallow. It usually proves to be rather entertaining. Some kids sit on their hands while others sing a song or avoid looking at the temptation.*

To discourage impulse buying, you need to be a good example. If you go to the store and really want a red hat (and you know it is an impulse), tell your kids how much you want that red hat, but you think it is an impulse so you are going to delay buying it for a week. Then a week later, go back to the store and look at the hat. Do you really want it? No, it was an impulse! Forgo the purchase and explain to your kids how you "saved money." To prove a point, literally set aside the money in the Family Savings Jar and explain to your kids that you avoided making a purchasing mistake.

Listed below are some other ideas for building your child's exposure to delayed gratification. Try several of them over the next six months.

- $ Grow a crystal or polish rocks. For fun, take before and after pictures so you can appreciate the transformation.

- $ Have your kids nurture an ant farm. How long does it take them to burrow all the way to the bottom?

- $ Make a bird feeder and place it by a window. Count the number of different birds fed at one time. How many different types do you see? Have your kids fill the feeder as one of their household duties.

- $ Build a terrarium, purchase an Amaryllis bulb, or grow a garden.

- $ Consider purchasing or finding a caterpillar and watch it turn into a butterfly.

- $ Paint by numbers.

- $ Go fishing.

- $ Complete a large jigsaw puzzle.

- $ Build a bonfire and make s'mores.

Chapter 26
Layaway

One thing we have strayed away from in America is the delayed gratification of layaway. We have replaced it with the instant gratification of credit cards, which has taken us down a regrettable path of getting what we want before we have enough money to take possession of the item. Layaway is simply an agreement between storeowners and their customers to purchase expensive goods. For example, my dad's high-end women's clothing store offered layaway. If someone wanted to buy several outfits, but it was more than they could afford at that time, no problem, they could put it in layaway. In simple terms, we would accept a small down payment and obtain some basic contact information. Once completed, we would run the purchase upstairs and quite literally set it aside in the layaway section, which was simply a rack to hold the items that had the shopper's name on it. Then, over the next several weeks or months, the person would come in and make payments on the purchase. Finally, the person would come in to make the last payment. Oh, the joy on customers' faces! As one employee collected the money, another employee would run upstairs for the goods the person worked so hard to purchase debt-free.

Anytime you deal with two parties coming together and exchanging goods and service for money, parameters need to be drawn. The most common way a transaction occurs is you enter a store, pay the merchant the agreed upon price immediately, and walk out with your merchandise. Outside of some restrictions for returns, the deal is simple and complete.

Recently, a reemergence of layaway has occurred at some large stores like Sears, J. C. Penney, and Kmart. With layaway, the merchants' cost increases as a result of slower payment, increased bookkeeping, the need for storage space, and the risk of shoppers changing their minds or not paying in full or on a timely basis. As a result, there are usually additional terms that must be accepted. The terms tend to address such things as minimum purchase amount, down payment amount, and a timeframe to pay the full amount due. Furthermore, conditions are created in the event that the customer changes their mind, such as the forfeit of their deposit, to offset the store's opportunity cost. This is because the merchandise was unavailable to sell to another customer while it was set aside in layaway.

Your MoneyBags Mission

If your kids are saving toward an expensive goal, consider introducing them to layaway if the item is on sale or is in high demand and will likely be sold out in the future. For this to work and not be a point of contention between you and your kids, you need to set some parameters, like the merchant. Consider the following:

$ Limit the number of items your child can have in layaway at any given time to one.

$ Your child must pay you 10% down, before you will purchase the item.

$ They must pay you a set amount from their allowance Spend money weekly until the balance is paid in full.

$ Your child is not allowed to take possession or play with the item until it is paid in full. If they are caught breaking this rule, penalize them a dollar or whatever amount seems fitting.

$ If your child changes their mind about wanting the item, you have a couple of options. First, if it is in a reasonable period of time (less than thirty days) and you can return the item, do so, but put the 10% deposit money in the Family Tax Kitty to cover the expense of your time, and give the balance of the money back to your child for another goal. However, if it has been a period greater than thirty days, it becomes a MoneyBags Moment. Tell your child that they will not receive the item and all the money paid will go into the Family Tax Kitty. As a parent and the official owner, you can return the item, give it to charity, or enjoy it yourself.

Chapter 27
Out of Sight, Out of Mind

As I get older, I love to hear the behind-the-scenes of stories that happened when I was younger. One such story is when MoneyBags and Imogene wanted to buy a car for my sister. My parents were against the idea because they felt she needed to have skin in the game. They knew she would appreciate the car more if she had to work to pay for a car versus having one given to her.

So, my family created a win-win solution, with a little help from Imogene's brother Ross, who was a part owner of the local bank (Chapter 18). The story was that MoneyBags and Imogene helped my sister with the down payment and co-signed the loan, but my sister had to make the monthly loan payments. Uncle Ross had the bank draft her loan payment coupons.

I remember my sister handling her monthly payments with no problem. However, one month she was short and asked her friend to lend her money for the car payment. It was important to my sister to not breach the agreement, and she took pride in finding a solution that did not require our parents to bail her out. She made that payment and reimbursed her friend. Eventually, the loan was paid off and she owned the car. Story over? Nope. Not even close.

Invest and forget

About ten years later, my sister decided to go back to college and needed money. She had already exhausted the education funds that our parents had set aside. Enter the secret, stage left: her car loan was a fake. MoneyBags and Imogene had purchased the car for her, with the help of my uncle Ross, who had created fake loan payment coupons. Her payments were actually directed into a savings account in her name. Money that had been set aside for a fake car loan years later became the unexpected pool of money for her education needs. The lesson: invest and forget.

Your MoneyBags Mission

Tell your kids a story (money-related or not) about something you forgot for a long time and then, *BAM*, you found it! Ask your kids if they have a similar story.

How did they feel when they lost it, or did they even notice? How did they feel when they unexpectedly found it?

A fun way to have your kids experience an unexpected surprise is to have them write a letter or make a card to send to themselves. In the letter, have them write what they are grateful for and what special traits they have that make them unique and special. To create a surprise to amplify their experience, secretly write a special note to them about why they are special to you. After three months or so, mail both letters or cards to your kids and watch their reaction when they receive snail mail with the kind words about their uniqueness.

Chapter 28
The Thrill of the Hunt!

My good friend Carlos shared with me one of his fondest childhood memories. Like mine, his memory also revolved around Christmas. When he was a little boy, he loved finding out ahead of time what he was getting for Christmas. To do this, he would search high and low for all of his Christmas gifts in their hiding spots. Once he found them, he would take a peek. If the presents were wrapped, that did not stop him. He would ever so carefully unwrap the presents, check them out, and with great precision rewrap the presents so on Christmas day he could shake the box and, before opening, say, "Thank you for the blue striped sweater!"

One year, his parents found him the perfect gift and were determined to make it the Christmas surprise of his life. It became a family sting operation to create elaborate clues for Carlos to find his present. His sisters created fun Christmas poems and riddles to help him find his next clue. The first poem was innocently in a box under the tree, stating something to the effect of, "'Tis the season of joy for our little boy, bundle up and grab your hat; the next clue is out back." So Carlos got dressed to find the next clue. He was sent outside in the snow to the back yard, then back inside the house, upstairs to the shower, downstairs to the basement, and so on. Finally, the last clue led him to the clothes dryer. Inside was a beautifully wrapped present. He found and unwrapped his surprise gift, his dream Lego

The joy of delayed gratification

Galaxy Cruiser, which he still has and treasures today. This Christmas present was the best gift he ever received because it was the first time he really experienced the joy of surprise and built-up excitement from delayed gratification. From that day forward, he stopped the pre-Christmas present hunting so that the big day would be a big day.

In financial terms, the thrill of the hunt can save you money. Many people, like one of my business partners, love to find a deal. He gets a thrill finding something of high quality at a great price. The joke around our office is that he has had all his toys (car, motorcycle, and boat) shipped to him piece by piece. Over the years, he has received in the mail a starter, blower motor, bug deflector, tire, tow package, and more. Obviously, this saves him money, but he loves the hunt of researching and scoping out good money opportunities, whether it is buying "stuff," picking a stock, finding the highest interest rate for saving money, or scoring the lowest interest rate when borrowing money. At the end of the day, when it comes to money, a little hunting can pay off.

Your MoneyBags Mission

Pull out your local paper or go online and look for the bank charging the lowest fixed interest rates on cars. Which bank has the highest interest rate? Ask your kids whether they would rather have a high interest rate or a low interest rate when borrowing money. Look to see which bank is paying the highest interest rate on savings. Which bank is paying the lowest? When it comes to saving money, do they want a high or low interest rate? (Interest is covered in more detail in Chapter 51.)

Think of a creative way to surprise your child by creating your own elaborate clue game. You can be as creative as Carlos's family by making funny poems and riddles to find the next clue, or, simply make it a scavenger hunt (go on the Internet for quick ideas). You can make the prize a gift card, tickets to the zoo, a picnic lunch, or their favorite dinner.

The U.S. government proved that they know all about the thrill of the hunt when they introduced the quarters that allowed all fifty states and six territories to have unique designs (you can see them all online). Overnight, people began collecting the various state coins. One clever item is a map of the country, with a slot to hold each of the quarters. Consider collecting the U.S. quarters with your kids. How long does it take for you to get all fifty-six? If you have multiple kids you can have them work as a team or, if you prefer, have a friendly competition.

Depending on the age of your children, consider watching the romantic comedy *Serendipity* as a family. In the movie, John Cusack plays Jonathan Trager, who randomly meets Sara, played by Kate Beckinsale. The two hit it off in an unexpected meeting. Since they are both in relationships with other people and Sara is a big believer in fate, she refuses to simply exchange phone numbers to stay in contact. Instead, she casts them out into the world by placing her phone number in a book and his on a five-dollar bill. The movie revolves around their hunt for the respective items. After the movie, talk about the excitement that Sara and Jonathan had when they finally found the book and five-dollar bill. Did your kids get a little adrenaline rush when they finally found the items? What things have you hunted for individually or as a family?

Lastly, consider creating a family quest. For example, I have a friend who loves pizza. Whenever he travels, he researches the local mom-and-pop pizza joints ahead of time and tries to find the absolute best pizza. For me, after I worked for Disney, I wanted all things Mickey. For years people loved to shop for me since they knew that, if it had Mickey Mouse on it, I would love it. It became a quest for my family to find me the most unique Mickey. Imogene won when she bought me a sterling-silver business cardholder, which I still carry today. So, take a few minutes to dream up your family quest, whether it is the best pancake house, a rare stamp, or a vintage car.

Chapter 29
Shopping With a Purpose

I am always baffled when I hear about shopaholics who consider shopping a form of therapy. These people did not grow up Gillespie! My mother was and is the worst about "car-napping." A typical scenario starts with her asking me to accompany her on an errand run, to help with bags and keep her company. She always prepares a list and rarely deviates. It is a hunt and she is focused. The thirty-minute trip that she promised takes half the day.

See, my mom, being the frugal and particular person she is, does not go to one cleaner, but two (one for my dad's shirts to be laundered and one for the dry cleaning). When she runs to the grocery store, she neglects to tell me that she goes to one store for the meat, the farmers' market for the vegetables, another store for toiletries, and yet another store for the odd-ball stuff she cannot find in the previous three stores.

Her decision making, which I have learned to never challenge, is from her experience with which stores carry the best product for the price. Furthermore, she has an iron stomach and neglects to feed me! Now that I am older and wise to her ways, I refuse to go shopping with her unless she promises to put lunch on her list. To this day, when she asks me to join her on an errand run, the theme song to *Gilligan's Island* starts running through my head, " . . . five passengers set sail that day, for a three-hour tour, a three-hour tour." As you know, the tour was way more than three hours, just like my mother's innocent little shopping trips.

Due to my aversion to shopping and all the negatives I associate with it, such as spending money, I am perplexed by how many people practice retail therapy. In Minnesota, the Land of 10,000 Lakes, it might be more appropriate to change our state motto to the Land of 10,000 Malls. It is no surprise to me that the second-largest mall in the United States is located here. The Mall of America is huge and includes tons of stores and an indoor theme park. To further fuel the fire, there is no sales tax on clothing in Minnesota, so your retail dollar goes a little further here.

Today, so many people have been conditioned to go shopping and buy "stuff" they don't need because they feel entitled, depressed, sad, lonely, or bored. If your kids see you handling your emotions this way, they will likely follow your pattern. These people, unlike my mother, don't have a list. They go to the mall with no purpose other than to buy stuff to make them feel better. Some of them feel the urge to shop because they had a tough day, work hard for their money, or are trying to "keep up with the Joneses." Whatever the reason, buying stuff won't fix the underlying problem.

If you know you use shopping to feel better, take a step back and ask yourself why. Is this behavior in line with your spending goals and budget? Is it becoming an issue? Do you have credit card debt due to shopping sprees? Do you have purchases that still have the tags and have never been worn or used? Do you hide, or lie to your spouse about things you have purchased? If you answer yes to any of these questions, take a step back and remember that your kids are sponges and will likely mimic your behavior in the future. Now is your MoneyBags Moment. It's time to break the cycle. The best way to change your behavior is to be aware and make a deliberate choice to react differently. If you feel depressed, lonely, or whatever triggers the need for shopping therapy, consider one of the following:

- $ Join a gym and take your kids with you to work out.

- $ Go for a run, bike ride, or have a friendly game of tennis.

- $ Crack open a jigsaw puzzle or board game for the whole family.

- $ Volunteer. Find a charity that can use your services, such as a homeless shelter.

$ Give blood.

$ Pick a point on the map an hour away and explore the surprise destination as a family.

$ Have everyone write a gratitude list.

$ Gather things you no longer use and donate to Goodwill or the Salvation Army.

There are many other things you can do to avoid shopping and spending money—what free or low-cost activities does your family enjoy?

What if you really do just enjoy spending time with friends and family shopping? Make it an event with a budget. For example, plan a quarterly shopping day, where you take your kids back-to-school shopping or go shopping with your friends. If you have budgeted $200 a month to spend on clothes, consider saving that money up for your quarterly trip and having $600 to spend. This way, you shop with a purpose and a budget. You still complete your goal in getting your kids clothes or spending time with your shopping friends. Fewer trips to the mall will lower your impulse buying.

Personally, I have a rule. If I am not planning to spend the money, I don't look, regardless of whether the item is a puppy, a car, a house, or clothing. So when you feel the urge, like Dorothy from the *Wizard of Oz*, click your heels three times and tell yourself, "There will always be new and shiny things; there will always be new and shiny things."

Your MoneyBags Mission

Consider having a garage sale twice a year. Find things that both you and your kids can place for sale. This is a good way to evaluate your clutter. As you are going through the process, write down on a piece of paper what you think you paid for the items, the estimated number of times it was used or worn, and how much you feel you could sell it for. This process is not to make you feel ashamed or embarrassed; it is the start of the realization that all this stuff does not give you long-term joy and costs lots of money.

Have your kids work the garage sale with you; let them work with the money and help determine prices. As you make sales, make sure to track each family member's contribution, i.e., little Johnny's toys sold and he made ten dollars. The money raised from the sale needs to go into the Family Savings Jar. At the end of the sale, package up all the stuff you didn't sell and give it to charity. Make sure to keep the receipt for your tax return. Explain to your kids that Uncle Sam appreciates people giving so much that most people receive a tax break on their tax return. If you itemize your taxes, show them your 1040 Schedule A and look for the gifts for charity section toward the bottom of the page. From the money that your kids raised, let's say it is $12, return 10% ($12 x .10 = $1.20) to them as a "tax break" from the Family Tax Kitty to put into their MoneyBags Savings.

Ask your kids about the experience. Did they have fun? What did they like? What didn't they like? Were they surprised at how much money was raised? Did they feel the price their stuff sold for was too high or too low? Was it worth the work? How did it feel to de-clutter and give things to people who have less than they do?

Chapter 30
The Importance of Integrity

H. Jackson Brown, Jr., is known for the moving statement, "Live so that when your children think of fairness and integrity, they think of you."

Over the years as a Certified Financial Planner, I've been sad to see the amount of negative emotions, such as embarrassment and shame, that can revolve around money. One of the most dangerous behaviors that can trigger negative emotions and shame is lying about money. By not having the utmost integrity, the whole financial process derails.

For example, if you apply for a loan, you will notice that the bank will ask you to disclose your financial information: assets, liabilities, proof of income, and your credit report. The reason they do this is that some people lie to obtain a loan they don't qualify for because they have a poor repayment history, no job, or their income is too low for the payment commitment.

Conversely, some financial institutions don't always disclose all the facts clearly, or create so many "hoops" that they set people up to fail. When trust is violated, a bad loan can occur by either party. Banks may lend money when people are not qualified, and as a result, these people fail to repay the loan. Furthermore, borrowers may pay extra fees or see their interest rate skyrocket since all of the "hoops" were not clearly disclosed.

On a personal side, I have witnessed people lying to their spouses about the amount of money they have spent on purchases or their credit card debt. This lack of integrity causes people to sabotage the trust in the relationship and avoid working on the deeper problem: why did they feel the need to buy things they know they cannot afford or did not agree to purchase as a couple? You will hear a "joke" from some women that they sneak in newly purchased clothes or shoes and hide them in the back of the closet so their husband does not see the shopping bag. It becomes a power or shame game. Their goal is to avoid being confronted about their purchases by their spouse. Men can be guilty of buying tools and hiding them in the garage. This lack of integrity is very destructive.

When it comes to your kids, make sure that they know the importance of integrity. The sooner you teach them, the better. The book *The 7 Habits of Highly Effective People* by Stephen R. Covey includes an exercise that has stayed with me. He recommends thinking about who would attend your funeral and what kind of a person they would say you were. If you are out of integrity and your big picture does not align with what you would like to see, you need to make changes now.

Teach your children the importance of honesty by being a good role model. If you have lied to your spouse, consider righting the situation going forward. You can choose to make a promise to yourself or take the extra step and come clean to your spouse and commit to being honest about purchases in the future. Honesty means being honest all the time; big or small, it all starts at home.

Your MoneyBags Mission

If you make a purchase and you notice the clerk or wait staff made an error in your favor, point it out to them and pay your fair amount of the purchase. Why not? You owe it and you were planning to pay for it anyway. If you find a wallet, call the person and return it with all contents intact. If you go to a restaurant, don't order one drink for six people to drink from since there are free refills; buy six different drinks. If it is not in your budget, then drink water. If you go to a fast-food restaurant and get a cup for water, make sure you only fill it with water at the beverage station, not pop. Don't sneak your teens into events as under thirteen so they are free versus paying for their rightful age.

As a family, consider watching the movie *Liar Liar*. In the movie, Fletcher (Jim Carrey) is an attorney and a divorced father. Fletcher's son is upset about his dad's constant lies and broken promises. Then Fletcher misses his son's birthday party. That night his son wishes that his dad could no longer tell lies. Magically, his wish comes true and Fletcher's life is turned upside down.

After watching the movie together, talk about the changes in Fletcher's life. Which Fletcher did your kids like better: the one who lied or the one who could only tell the truth? Fletcher was also unable to tell white lies. Explain to your kids what a white lie is, and how they can say things honestly but nicely without telling white lies.

Chapter 31
Following the Rules

My favorite sport is volleyball and I play it several days a week. One thing that makes me chuckle is my girlfriend who is a stickler for following the rules. As she puts it, you don't follow SOME of the rules, you follow ALL of the rules. Often, she can gain a point by challenging referees when they are lax.

When it comes to money, following the rules pays off. So, what are the rules? They're simple: what did you promise? If you take out a loan, you promised to make timely payments, monthly, with interest until the loan is paid back. For example, if you take out a car loan for $20,000 with a 4.75% interest rate for five years, then you promise to pay $374 on the fifteenth of the month until it is paid off.

The cheapest and smartest way to accomplish your goal is to do exactly what you promised, or pay it off faster, assuming there is no prepayment penalty.

When you are late in making your payment, this disappoints the lender, which has a negative impact on you. They will charge a late fee, and if you are thirty days late, they will report it to the credit agencies. Negative reporting to credit agencies will make borrowing money in the future more expensive, since it will lower your credit score and show up as a blemish on your credit report. One win/win arrangement that several banks use is giving a lower interest rate if you establish an automated payment from your checking account. Every month the bank will automatically pull the payment directly from your checking account, and you get a lower interest rate and avoid late payments.

Your MoneyBags Mission

If you have a loan, consider looking at your online or paper loan statement with your kids. When are the payments due? Look at the history. Have your payments been paid on time or have they been late? Were you charged late fees? How do you pay your loans? Are they automated so you are not late or do you send the payments in the mail, which takes away the certainty of when a payment will be received?

Over the next couple of weeks, focus on following ALL of the rules. If the express lane in the supermarket says ten items and you have twelve, then go to the regular lane. Recycle all bottles, papers, and cans. Make sure to silence your cell phone when you go to the movie theater. Work on your table manners; don't start eating until everyone is seated and served, don't talk with your mouth full, no phone calls or texting at the table, say please and thank you, ask to be excused, and so on.

Do what you promised

There are a couple of fun card games that demonstrate the importance of knowing the rules by always changing the rules. Both games work best with three or more players. One is called Fluxx, by Loony Labs. The game starts by dealing three cards out to everyone. Then you draw a card and play a card until the rules change, which will happen quickly. A more traditional game is Uno by Mattel.

Chapter 32
Your Word is Law

Two things I enjoy about my family are that we have a great sense of humor, and our word is law. Years ago, my dad managed a department store and the company gave his store a fundraising goal of $10,000. My dad wanted to motivate his employees to give money to the charity. To set a safety net for himself and make it worth his "pain" in stepping out of his comfort zone, he told the employees that if they raised $12,500, he would dress as a woman for a day. Once the bar was set, the buzz in the store began with the goal to have him "put his money (skirt) where his mouth is."

Sure enough, at the end of the fundraising time period, they exceeded the stretch goal. Keeping to his word, he proudly dressed as a six-foot-two woman for the day. I am sure some people would have been embarrassed if they had to follow through with this promise, but not my father. He hammed up the day. His employees dressed him and applied his makeup. He was visible, talked to customers, and explained how proud he was of his employees in surpassing the store's fundraising goal. Not only did he encourage these people to raise money for a good cause, but because of his stunt he also got them wonderful public relations—a picture with a story ran in the local paper the following day and appeared in the company newsletter.

The financial system is based on promises

Teach your kids that their word is law. In other words, they need to learn to keep their promises. This ties into money because the entire financial system is based on promises. For example, when you take out a loan, you have promised the person or financial institution that lent you the money that you will pay them back, no matter what the circumstance. If you don't agree to that, then why should they lend you money? Hence, if you take out a student loan and don't finish your degree, you still owe the bank the money you borrowed. If you take out a car loan and it drops in value, gets destroyed in a car crash, or is stolen, this is not the bank's problem; it is your problem. You still owe the bank the remainder of the loan balance, which is why you purchase insurance.

Your MoneyBags Mission

For fun, have your kids imagine a perfect world where everyone keeps their promises. What would it be like . . . if their favorite uncle tells them he will take them to Hawaii when they graduate from high school, and actually does? If their teacher makes a deal that he will shave his head if they read ten books in four weeks, and he follows through? Think of other circumstances where it would be cool if people kept their word.

Now, imagine a world where no one keeps their promises. In the classic comic strip "Peanuts," Lucy, a smart brunette, always lies to Charlie Brown. One memorable, recurring scene is Charlie asking Lucy to hold a football for him so he can punt the ball. Just as he is about to kick the ball, she pulls the ball away, causing Charlie to fall. What would it be like if everyone pulled a Lucy? In my story about my dad, how disappointing would it have been had he not followed through with his promise? Imagine the people who gave more money than they had planned just to see the "show." When have you or your kids been disappointed about someone not following through with their promise? How did it feel? Do you lose trust on future agreements?

What if your family planned to take a trip to Walt Disney World, but when you arrived at the airport, they said your tickets were no good and nonrefundable? What if you rented a car and drove to Disney, only to find that the tickets you had purchased at a discount for the Magic Kingdom were no longer honored? How would that make you feel? As a family, think of how the world would be if you could not trust the word of a person or a business.

Going forward, focus on making promises and carrying them out. For example, if you promise to take the kids for ice cream if they are good for the day, then make sure to follow through. If your kids don't listen when you tell them to stop running in the house or they will lose their TV privileges, keep your word. If your kids promise to clean up their rooms, then make sure they honor their promises.

Another way to approach this is how a good friend of mine handles it in her family. She tells her kids she will not make a promise unless she can keep her word. Instead, she lets them know she will try or see how things work out so she doesn't have to go back on her word. This way, she does not get into the habit of making promises she cannot keep. As a result, when she makes a promise, her kids know they can count on it happening.

Chapter 33
Respectful and Responsible to Things

Spend a short period of time in my mother's kitchen and you will see someone who respects and is responsible to things, almost to a fault. When I return home for the holidays, my family and I have fun ribbing my mom about being frugal. She still has the same wooden spoon that is now splintered. Not to mention her tattered potholders, over-sharpened knifes, electric grill that is older than me, and an electric mixer that was a wedding gift from 1965.

It is her frugal side that has allowed her to save money. Her beloved tattered potholders that grip well save her money every day that she uses them. For example, let's say a good way to grade a "good" purchase is that, from the time you buy something to the time you decommission the item, it costs you only a penny a day. Note, this assumes you actually use it and it is not off in a corner accumulating dust like most peoples' exercise equipment. So if my Mom purchased her potholders for $5 and used them every day for 500 days ($5.00 / 500 = $0.01) she would have made a good purchase and could be guilt-free if she threw them away. However, it is likely that she bought them 20 years ago. So, if she used them every day for the last 20 years (365 days x 20 years = 7,300), she got 7,300 uses

How do you judge a good purchase?

out of those potholders. Now, divide the $5 cost by the number of uses ($5 / 7,300 = $0.000685) to get the cost per use. In other words, not only did she get 7,300 uses, but she continues to save money by using them beyond the expected lifecycle. Let's say she had replaced them every 2 years and they cost $5 each time, she would have spent $50 versus her actual $5 (20 years / 2 year lifecycle = 10 replacements at $5 x 10 = $50).

My mother, the ultimate cook, benefits two ways. First, she saves money by making every purchase last well beyond the expected lifecycle. In addition, she did not spend money replacing items, so she can redirect the money to savings or to expanding her array of kitchen utensils.

Your MoneyBags Mission

Go through the exercise above with some of your household items. Look for new items you have purchased and figure out how many days you would have to own and use them so they only cost you a penny a day. Pick items that are both yours and your kids, new and old, expensive and cheap. Are you close to the penny-a-day goal? Does it seem impossible?

Consider the same exercise as above, but do it on your car and the number of miles you have on your odometer. For example, if your car cost $30,000, how many miles do you have to drive it for it to only cost a dollar per mile ($30,000 / $1 = 30,000 miles)? How many miles do you need to drive it to drop the cost to $0.50 a mile ($30,000 / $0.50 = 60,000 miles)? If you place 200,000 miles on your car, how much will it cost you per mile ($30,000 / 200,000 = $0.15)? How many miles do you need to drive it to get down to the penny per mile mark ($30,000/$0.01 = 3,000,000)? Do you think your car will make it?

As your children make purchases with their own money, encourage them to do some calculating to see how long they can make their purchase last. If they saved up and purchased a $50 toy, encourage responsible behavior by rewarding your child if they have not lost or broken the toy by the $0.50 mark ($50 /$0.5 = 100 days) by giving them a 5% rebate on the one hundredth day ($50 x $0.05 = $2.50). If they get to the $0.25 mark (200 days), give them another 5% rebate! An easy way to do this is to place the receipt in an envelope and put it in the Family Savings Jar. The receipt has the date and price printed on it for easy record keeping. Quarterly, review the receipt and see if you have crossed the bonus mark.

My favorite all-time homework assignment that teaches responsibility is to parent an egg. I am not sure what teacher started this one, but it is brilliant. The goal is to teach kids about babies, but I feel you should start at a younger age to teach overall responsibility. The task is to take an egg and have your kids carry it with them everywhere they go for a week. For younger kids, start for a couple hours and work up over time. The kids can have fun with the egg by coloring it and naming it. However, you need to treat it like a baby. I recommend making this an annual tradition, a rite of passage, or form of initiation to prepare for purchasing an expensive product. For example, if your kid wants to purchase a cell phone and has saved the money, the last step before purchasing that phone is to pass a one-week egg test.

Rules:

$ The child is not allowed to carry the egg inside a plastic baggie to reduce the mess if it breaks; if this were a baby, it would suffocate.

$ The child cannot hard-boil the egg—you just killed the baby.

Respectful and Responsible to Things

$ The child cannot leave the egg unattended.

$ The child can hire and pay an egg sitter (maximum four hours a day—great time to practice bartering Chapter 46).

$ The child can let the egg nap two hours a day and sleep for eight hours a night in a safe location.

$ A parent needs to sign or mark the egg with a permanent marker to ensure no switching of the egg.

$ If the egg breaks during the test, wait a week, then pick a new egg and start the initiation clock over.

$ If the child successfully cares for the egg for the entire week: congratulations! The child has your blessing to make their dream purchase!

Chapter 34
Penny Wise and Pound Foolish

Entrepreneurs are wired to cut expenses. MoneyBags was the king of thrifty, so much that it was common for him to be penny wise and pound foolish (P&P). One day when he was working at Ned's Shed, he needed to order more drinking cups. To do so required a long-distance phone call to his supplier. To save a few pennies by avoiding the expensive long distance call, he went to great lengths.

It started with a local call to my uncle Joe, who took over my great grandfather's monument business. We all lovingly laughed at and respected Joe's low technology radio system that allowed him to stay connected with the different branches in the tri-state area at no cost. MoneyBags asked Joe if he would use his employees, via the radio network, to contact the cup company to place the order. So my uncle radioed one branch that in turn radioed another branch, which then made the local toll-free call to the cup company to place the order for MoneyBags. Then, the communication train turned around. The person who placed the order radioed back to the branch, and so on, to let my grandfather know the order was placed. So, instead of being efficient and making one long-distance phone call to place the order, MoneyBags involved another business and three other employees' time, which cost everyone more money in the long run.

Teach your kids to think ahead to avoid being P&P. This covers a gamut of things from insurance to maintenance. For example, cars need maintenance on a regular basis to keep them running smoothly. Some people skip having their oil changed. They don't make it a priority or they don't have the $20 for the oil change. Months down the road they could burn up their engine because they did not change the oil. Now, they have a $3,000 repair bill!

Another example is when people don't go to the dentist to have their teeth cleaned every six months because it is expensive or they hate going to the dentist. Well, a $125 semiannual cleaning bill is a lot less painful and less expensive than spending $800 on fillings or even more for a root canal! How about people who drive all across town to buy the cheapest gas, but spend both time and gas to save a buck? Do you know people who don't purchase health insurance because it is expensive ($200 to $500 a month), even though one broken leg or surgery could cost tens of thousands of dollars?

To determine if you are being P&P, evaluate whether your savings strategy is saving you money or costing you money. To start, set a monetary value for an hour of your labor. A good gauge is to use the amount that your employer pays you hourly. For kids, use their weekly allowance. Once you set your hourly rate, evaluate if a task is saving or costing you money. For example, if your hourly rate is $20, and it takes you three hours to complete the task versus paying someone $200 to complete the same job, then you saved money ($20 x 3 = $60, $200 - $60 = $140 saved). Conversely, let's assume the same task and hourly rate, but you had to purchase $100 in parts and it took you thirty hours over several weekends ($20 x 30 = $600, $600 + $100 = $700 cost, $700 - $200 = $500 lost time). Therefore, it would be cheaper and faster to pay someone to do the task.

Your MoneyBags Mission

Take a fun look at your family: what odd things do you do that are P&P? Have your kids help you make a list of your silly habits that might be P&P, then go through the steps above to calculate whether they are P&P.

Over the next week, look for examples on TV (sitcoms are usually the best spot) to find people being P&P. Make a game of it, like Slug Bug, where you playfully punch someone in the arm and say "P&P, P&P!" in a funny voice!

In the future, when you evaluate doing a project yourself or hiring it out, make sure to do a quick calculation to see if it is saving you money or actually costing you money.

Chapter 35
Coupons!

I have fond memories of my mother and her coupons. She would go through papers, cutting out coupons and storing them in a tattered envelope that she carried in her purse. My mother, the ever-so-detailed bookkeeper, would set aside the money that she actually saved from using the coupons. After she accumulated so much money, she would treat herself to some purchase she wanted. One of her splurges occurred when we were skiing in Colorado. As we were walking through the village, she found a beautiful brass kaleidoscope that she obviously did not need, but wanted. I remember her justifying the purchase, since she was using her "coupon money." I don't remember the exact amount of the kaleidoscope, but I would guess $100. To this day, when I go home I admire that kaleidoscope, and I remember that moment.

Over the years I have noticed that not all people handle coupons the same way as my mom. Recently, extreme couponing has not only become the "in thing," but it is also a reality TV show. I have seen many people get roped into buying things they don't need or want, but they cannot resist a "great deal." For example, using a coupon for 50% off snow tires when you live in Florida, or stockpiling diapers when you don't have a baby. Some people get so excited to "spend less" via using a coupon that they buy ten tomatoes when they only need one. This causes them to have to give away the unneeded tomatoes or let them spoil. Having a coupon does not mean you should use it.

A point of clarity—money is not actually "saved" unless you set it aside like my mother. Otherwise you just "spent less," which is good, but not the same as SAVING MONEY!

Your MoneyBags Mission

Take some time out as a family to look through your mail or online for money saving opportunities, such as coupons, rebates, and discounts. Equate looking for these savings opportunities as panning for gold—coupon gold. Often you can find coupons for everyday items that the family uses, like soap, bread, and milk. Sometimes, places offer discounts if you bring your own containers, like reusable shopping bags or coffee cups. Others provide reward cards that give you gas discounts once you have spent a certain dollar amount or give you ten cents off a cup of coffee for answering a trivia question correctly. Several restaurants run daily specials, reward loyal customers via punch cards, or give discounts for completing a quick online survey.

As you uncover the different opportunities, focus on the offers that the family will directly benefit from versus getting distracted by the size of the discount. For example, if your family regularly eats bagels, and you see a buy-one-get-one free for your favorite brand, consider this *coupon gold!* When you save money via coupon gold, do as my mom did and put the money saved in your Family Savings Jar. Conversely, if you see a coupon that makes no sense for the family, such as buy ten cans of wasp spray to save a dollar in the middle of winter, consider this *fools' gold.* Don't be fooled by it. Simply treat it like a "hot potato" and get rid of it as fast as possible.

Chapter 36
Understanding Risk

When I was growing up, Evel Knievel was the ultimate risk taker! He was always on his motorcycle jumping cars, with his ultimate goal jumping the Grand Canyon. One thing that I have learned over the years is that there are varying degrees of risk. Evel was on the crazy wild end of risk taking. On the other end of the risk spectrum is Samuel Jackson's character Elijah in the movie *Unbreakable*. Elijah has extremely brittle bones that break under the slightest strain so he takes several precautions to avoid this.

In order to be smart with money, you need to understand risk and its tradeoffs. Risk is simply the odds that something negative is going to happen. There is risk in everything we do. The best example of the difficulty in trying to avoid risk is in the movie *Rain Man*. Dustin Hoffman's character Ray is at the airport with his brother Charlie, played by Tom Cruise. Ray refuses to get on a plane since he can recite when each airline experienced a crash. Charlie finally gives up and decides to drive to Los Angeles, but Ray knows about traffic accidents too. At one point, out of desperation, Charlie agrees to allow Ray to walk. The tradeoff for Ray's need for safety is a much longer commute. Imagine how long it would take if you wanted to walk from New York City to Los Angeles.

Investments have similar risks. If you are so scared to lose money, then the amount that you can make on your investment will decrease greatly and will increase the time you need to reach your goal. The first step in making money is to know and understand your risks. Then you have to decide if you are willing to accept the odds of the downside of the risk happening to you. If so, you have three options when it comes to risk and investing: proceed, limit your exposure by decreasing the amount of your investment, or avoid the investment.

Your MoneyBags Mission

As a family, discuss modern or historical figures who took risks, such as Pilgrims, revolutionaries, investors, civil-rights activists, military personnel, firemen, or police officers.

$ What risks did they take?

$ Why do you think they felt the risk was worth taking?

$ What do you think were their deciding factors?

$ What are specific risks each member of the family thinks they would consider taking or not taking and the reasoning behind each decision?

$ Ask your kids what one risk-taker (living or dead) they would most like to have dinner with. Why?

$ What questions would they like to ask their dinner guest?

Take this opportunity to explain a risk you took and its outcome, or describe a risk you regret not taking. Ask your children what specific risks they would take or avoid and their reasoning behind their decisions.

For fun, see what your kids' risk tolerance for money is and discuss their rationales. Ask them where they would choose to put their money: in a safe place where there is no chance to lose and they make a guaranteed 2% a year, or in an investment that could earn them an average of 10% a year, but has a 20% chance of dropping to zero?

Depending on the age of your children, consider watching the movie *Unbreakable*. Look for the precautions Samuel Jackson's character Elijah takes to avoid breaking his bones. Talk about the different risks that Elijah took, such as driving his car. What did he do to reduce his exposure to broken bones? When you ride in a car, what safety precautions do you and your kids take to reduce the risk of broken bones? How would their perception of risk change if they were Bruce Willis's character David? What would you do differently if you were David?

For the next week, analyze the risk of things you do. For example, if you go out to eat, what are the risks of bad things happening to you? You could get food poisoning, the place could be robbed, or your service could be lousy. Conversely, what good things could happen? You could see a famous person, the food could be out of this world, you could find out your server is your long-lost cousin, or you could get a free meal since you are the ten thousandth customer. When it comes to spending money on "stuff," what are the tradeoffs?

Ask your kids if they would do the following. What are the pros and cons?

- **$** Run a marathon?
- **$** Read one hundred books in a year?
- **$** Play tennis on a hot summer day?
- **$** Go skiing in a blizzard?
- **$** Skydive?
- **$** Bungee jump?
- **$** Hold a snake?
- **$** Spend $100 on a cell phone?

PART 3
MoneyBags Mechanics and Skills . . .
How Money Works

Pennies, Nickels, and Dimes!

Chapter 37
The Value of a Penny

Being from the state of Illinois, Land of Lincoln, I have always loved the penny. Abraham Lincoln is engraved on the front, and it is the only copper-plated coin, so it stands out from the others. To date, Illinois still accepts pennies in their toll booths!

When I was growing up, I would find a penny and yell, "Find a penny, pick it up, all day long I will have good luck!" As I got a little older, some of my friends would tell me to pass it by and only pick it up if it was heads up, since they thought tails up was bad luck. Gratefully, by that time, I was too ingrained in my habits to walk away, so I kept picking them up. Now, I see people just walk by and tell me they are not worth picking up. What!?

Years ago you could buy a piece of gum, but today nothing costs a penny. As a result, many people don't

**Find a Penny
pick it up**

think pennies should be coined anymore. Stop this crazy line of thinking and teach your children the value of the smallest denomination—a penny. I am amazed that so many people never bend over to pick up a penny. If it was your job to pick up a penny every second, your hourly rate would be $36 (60 seconds x 60 minutes = 3,600 pennies / 100 = $36 an hour) or $74,880 for the year ($36 x 40 hours a week x 52 weeks a year). Not bad!

Your MoneyBags Mission

For fun, have your kids calculate how much money they would have if they found and saved a penny a day for the next five years? ($0.01x 365 days x 5 years = 1,825 pennies + $0.01 for leap year = 1,826, 1,826 / 100 = $18.26)

T. Harv Eker, author of the *Secrets of the Millionaire Mind: Mastering the Inner Game of Wealth*, takes finding money to a laughable level, since he encourages everyone around him to dive for loose change on the ground, pick it up, and announce that they are a "Money Magnet." As a family, adopt this ritual and imagine the memories you can create with your kids. Similar to the money hunt game discussed in Chapter 4, consider randomly dropping change around your house and driveway for your kids to find so they can immediately experience and shout out that they are Money Magnets!

Chapter 38
Counting Money

One day I was home for a visit and I asked my niece Paige how much money she had in her piggy bank. She told me, "A lot, but I don't like to count it." This response surprised me. Unlike Paige, I was exposed to the counting of money often, due to my dad's business. To me it was a daily task. After my shock wore off, I had her run upstairs, grab her piggy bank, and bring it down to count. I took great joy in dumping all of her money on the kitchen table. I then showed her how to organize stacks of the coins so it would be easy to count.

To count money, make sure to use a table, which is easier and faster than the floor, since you can slide the coins off the table versus trying to pick them up; plus the piles don't fall over like they can on carpet. To create stacks quickly, slide the coins off the table into your other hand. Then when you have the desired amount, do a little shake, shake, shake to get them to line up in your hand so you can load the stack back onto the table using your hand like a giant claw releasing the coins. Don't forget to throw in sound effects.

Start easy by counting the quarters and putting in them in stacks of four to equal $1. Then dimes (10 = $1), nickels (10 = $0.50), pennies (10 = $0.10), and stacks totaling $1 in odd coins (half dollars and the remaining pennies, nickels, dimes, and quarters). Put the stacks in columns five deep and then drop down to create another row.

Your MoneyBags Mission

Now that your kids have been saving money, tell them to grab their piggy banks and dump them out on the kitchen table. If you have multiple kids, keep their piles separate. Help them make the piles, but let them do most of the work. As you are digging through the money, look for unique coins. Do you have any wheat-back pennies? Buffalo nickels? How many different state quarters can you find? Once done, have them count the Family Savings Jar and the Tax Kitty. Which jar has the most money?

Money has a very distinct smell. Once you are done, have your kids smell their hands. Explain to them that the smell is from all of the people who have touched the money plus the combination of metal and dust . . . Okay, now have them run and wash their hands.

To go a step further, teach your kids how to roll coins. You can purchase the needed supplies at any office supply store. When you have a good amount, to the point where you are going to be slightly embarrassed to hand it over to a teller, take the money to the bank with your children and let them see how the teller handles the money. Once the teller tells you the amount you have accumulated, great! Keep it earmarked for your goal!

Note: *Sometimes you see public change machines that charge a fee, or the bank may have a machine in the lobby. Most of them require you to undo all your hard work and unroll the coins. Explain to your children that they do this because some Takers try to defraud the machines by putting things like metal washers in the rolls instead of coins.*

Chapter 39
Counting Money Back

Most people have warm, fuzzy memories of their grandmothers cooking wonderful meals in the kitchen. Not me. My main job when Imogene came up for a visit was to keep her out of my mother's kitchen. However, what she lacked in cooking skills, she made up for by being the ultimate saleswoman. She ran my father's store in their hometown with a simple cash draw and no technology. It was fun to watch her make a sale, write the receipt, and count the cash back. She never needed a calculator.

In fact, no one in my family had trouble making change, since we were taught at an early age. Not many kids grow up with an old manual cash register in their garage, but I did. My sister and I made a game out of "running the store." Nothing was better than hearing the manual click, click, click, of the keys and the sound the handle made when you pulled it down, combined with the reward of the cash draw opening! Every time I hear the beginning of the song "Money" by Pink Floyd, I think of that register with its cool sounds and I smile.

It is important to teach your kids how to count money back. This technique is actually pretty easy, but so rarely used due to the advances of technology. Most of us just trust we are getting the proper money back and never check. If the power is down and no calculators are available, you can see a look of horror in most cashiers' faces when they have to make change, especially if they have coins given to them to even up a bill.

Your MoneyBags Mission

Teach your kids how to count money back. To do so, always start with the change and get it to a nickel, dime, quarter, or dollar as quickly as possible. Once done, add in the bills. For example, if the purchase is $3.92 and the cashier receives $10, start with $0.92, you need $0.03 (count $0.93, $0.94, $0.95) to get to $0.95. Then add a nickel to get to a whole dollar (count $4). Add $1 (count $5) to get to $5; add a five-dollar bill (count $10) to complete the count back to $10. The amount of change needed is $6.08.

Occasionally, cashiers run into "change avoiders." These people give the exact amount of change owed to reduce their change. Apparently they don't have a Family Savings Jar that they want to fill up. Giving them the proper change back is easy since the coins cancel out the change, so you can simple drop cents from the equation. Now you just need to pay back bills. For example, if the bill is $11.27 and you are given $20.27, it is as if the bill is only $11, since the coins cancel the change, thus you give back $9. Count back four singles $12, $13, $14, $15, and then add a five-dollar bill to get $20.

Over the next week, when you go to a store or restaurant, keep the receipts. When you return home, have your kids pretend to be the cashier. They will need a "drawer" of money to work with. You can use play money or change from your Family Savings Jar. If you went to the grocery store and spent $37.52, hand your child $40 or $50 and have them make you change.

Chapter 40
Tipping

Years ago I went with a group of friends to an Italian restaurant, and we had the best waiter in the world; his nickname was Cupcake! That night we had so much fun. He told us jokes, gave us superb recommendations on the menu, and excellent service. It was as if we were his only and favorite table in the entire restaurant. At the end of the night, we wanted to show our appreciation for having him as our waiter, so we made sure to leave him a BIG TIP as a thank you for a job well done.

Cupcake and his service was the concept in mind when they created the word TIPS, which is actually an acronym "To Insure Prompt Service." Certain occupations such as wait staff, cab drivers, bellhops, hairdressers, and valet parking staff receive tips when providing excellent service. Since tipping is in so many facets of life, it is important to teach your children about tipping. First, teach them to think ahead and be aware if they are likely to be in a tipping situation, such as when eating out, in an airport, in a hotel, or getting valet parking, so they are prepared with cash on hand. Many times you can tip via a credit card, but cash is better for some tipping situations.

Next, you need to know the going rate for tipping. Usually, for services where people wait on you for a period of time (wait staff, hairdresser, cab driver, or spa service), you tip anywhere from 10 to 20%. If you feel the service was poor, tip 10% (or less); adequate 15%; and Cupcake level 20% (or more). For what I call the "crossing my path" tip (bellhop and valet), where they simply were in your route from point A to point B, you usually tip $1 per bag, or a couple of bucks for their service. Some people also tip hotel and cruise housekeeping $2 to $5 dollars a night.

Tipping has a few hidden pitfalls. First, don't tip on tax; look for the subtotal and calculate the tip from that total. When you are in a large party at restaurants, many times the tip or gratuity is already added to your bill. Therefore, don't add on top of the calculated gratuity, unless you really want to compliment the wait staff. Third, when you receive a special deal, such as a coupon or buy-one-get-one-free, tip the wait staff based on the whole price you would have been charged, not the amount less the discount. Lastly, tipping customs vary greatly in different countries, so do a little research when traveling.

Your MoneyBags Mission

When you go on a trip or to the city, teach your children to think ahead about the amount of cash they will need. For example, if you are going on vacation and you are going to park your car in the long-term lot, take a courtesy shuttle to the airport where the driver helps you with your bags, and check six bags with the skycap, determine how much cash you will likely need and then bring a little extra.

When you go to restaurants, have your kids figure out the tip. If the bill is $40 plus $3.50 tax, have them calculate in 10%, 15%, and 20% tips. Was the service outstanding? Do you want to tip high? If you need help, the next chapter covers easy ways to calculate tips.

Chapter 41
The Importance of Ballpark Numbers

In the movie *Rain Man*, I am always impressed when Dustin Hoffman's character Ray knows *exactly* how many toothpicks fell on the floor, in the blink of an eye. I always think how cool it would be to have that ability. Can you imagine looking at a jar of jelly beans or glancing at a stadium of stairs and knowing the exact number of beans and steps?

Thankfully, as a Certified Financial Planner, being exact to the penny is not important, but being close counts. When people ask me what the difference is between what I do compared to accountants or tax preparers, I jokingly tell them that I like really large round numbers. Unlike accountants or tax preparers who work most of the time with facts, in my world the numbers are moving every day due to the stock market, clients' spending or saving their money, and shifting assumptions. So estimating a ballpark number is just as good as knowing the exact number. In fact, in my line of business, it is better since it saves time.

Teach your kids how to use ballpark math. Nothing impresses me more than when a client of mine can estimate or do math quickly in their head.

Your MoneyBags Mission

Practice estimating numbers. Listed below are a few tricks.

Yearly Calculations:

In the financial world, almost everything is based on annual numbers, but information is received in many forms, such as hourly or monthly. Therefore, it helps to quickly get the numbers to an annual ballpark number. For example, if a person can save $500 a month, a fast way to estimate (if you haven't memorized the multiples of 12) is to multiply the amount by 10 ($500 x 10 = $5,000) and then double the remaining 2 months ($500 x 2 = $1,000). Thus, they can save $6,000 a year ($5,000 + $1,000 = $6,000).

Go through your budget and have your kids estimate your monthly expenses to annual. If you have not reviewed your budget in a while, now is a great time to update it.

Hourly Rates:

If someone gives you their annual income, a quick way to determine a ballpark hourly rate is to take the thousands and divide by 2. For example, if someone makes $50,000, the estimated hourly rate is $25 (50 / 2 = $25, long hand $50,000 / 26 weeks / 80 hours = $24.04).

Percentages:

To calculate the sale price, if you have an item that costs $150 and it is 50% off, you can divide by two. You can also break it down by taking half of $100 ($50) and half of $50 ($25), to calculate that it will cost only $75 ($50 + $25 = $75).

To quickly estimate ballpark numbers when tipping, for example on a $125 bill, move the decimal point over one place to the left for a 10% tip ($12.50) or double the 10% tip to create a 20% tip ($12.50 x 2 = $25). To calculate 15%, take the 10% tip ($12.50) and divide by 2 ($12.50 / 2 = $6.25) and add it back to the 10% ($12.50 + $6.25 = $18.75). Often people will simply round up to $19.

As discussed in the previous chapter, when you go to restaurants, have your kids practice calculating the tip. When you are running errands, have your kids estimate tax and calculate discounts on items.

For fun, fill a jar full of jelly beans and have your kids ballpark the number of jelly beans in the jar. See how creative they get. A common way to estimate the number is to lift the jar and count the number of jelly beans on the bottom. Then, count the number of rows from the bottom to the top and multiply. Try it with your kids and see how close you are. What was more fun, coming up with a ballpark number or counting them one by one?

Chapter 42
The Importance of Having Your Kids WORK for What They Want

According to *The Millionaire Next Door* by Thomas J. Stanley, Ph.D. and William D. Danko, Ph.D., millionaires want their children to have better lives than they had, so they encourage them to go to school and discourage them from working at an early age. Unknowingly, they are discouraging frugality, the trait that made them millionaires, and indirectly encouraging high consumption (spending), a behavior that will hinder their children's future financial success.

Teach your kids to work for things they want. When I was a Brownie, I sold the famous Girl Scout cookies. I remember one girl in my troop always sold tons of cookies each year, always winning the biggest prize. I never dreamed of reaching her level. I thought it was

an impossible amount of cookies to sell. To this day, I am not sure how she did it, but I am confident that she raised this money all on her own with pure tenacity.

Likewise, I raised the money on my own. My parents never took my cookie list into work asking employees or co-workers to buy them. However, they would take me into my dad's store so I had the opportunity to sell to people I knew. They would also encourage me to go door to door in our neighborhood and personally ask for sales. When the cookies came, don't think for a moment that my mom drove me around the neighborhood. I had to go door to door pulling a wagon to deliver them.

The amazing thing is fourfold. First, I was the only one responsible for the number of cookies I sold or did not sell. Second, it was my first sales experience. At an early age I learned the importance of overcoming my nervousness in approaching and asking people for their purchase. Few people say no to a cute little Brownie, so it is super safe training ground. Third, I learned about sales incentives. There was always a clearly laid-out incentive plan, so I knew how many boxes of cookies I needed to sell to reach my desired prize. Lastly, I found out that there was a direct correlation between the number of people I asked and the number of cookies I sold. Like the girl in my troop, I always wanted to get something for my efforts (I just did not shoot as high as she did—she always outsold me in the fruit fundraiser for our band, too).

When your kids have fundraisers, encourage them to raise the money. Don't do it for them. If they don't feel it is important, why are you paying the bill for them to be in that activity? They need to approach people and ask them to make a purchase (sales). They need to record the order (bookkeeping). They need to collect the money (responsibility), thank the buyer (relationship building), and deliver the goods (accountability). Lastly, they need to always set a goal (reward).

Your MoneyBags Mission

A fun game for the family to work on everyone's sales skills is the card game Snake Oil by Out of the Box Publishing. The game works best with several players. One person draws an occupation card and everyone else has to create what they feel that player will need by combining two of the word cards in their hand. Be ready for some zany products and outrageous pitches to sell products!

One way to teach your kids to work for what they want is to cook from scratch. My mom is an excellent cook and I appreciate her teaching me how to cook. This allows your kids to reap the rewards from their hard work. Plus, when cooking from scratch, you will dirty the kitchen and lots of dishes. The cleanup is part of the work you want your kids to share and experience.

Some of my favorite memories of making food from scratch with my mom are things you can do, too:

- **$** Make a pie or homemade pizza, including the dough, from scratch.

- **$** Go to an orchard and pick strawberries, tomatoes, or apples to clean and eat or use in a pie, jam, or sauce.

- **$** On a hot summer day, consider making homemade ice cream and have your kids manually churn the ice cream. I bet the homemade ice cream is ten times better than the store-bought kind because they enjoyed having a hand in the creation.

Finally, to gauge your child's commitment to extra-curricular activities, have them create a game plan to raise money for their goal. For example, if they want to attend a certain camp, such as horseback-riding camp, have them create a plan to raise the money. Maybe they mow lawns, babysit, help you paint, or clean out the garage. Once the plan is created, they can do a small presentation to the family. Make sure to praise them for their efforts and help them in areas where they are weak. This is also a time for you to consider helping them with matching funds. For example, if they raise 50%, maybe you match them 50%.

Chapter 43
Profit

Every chance you get, talk to your kids about profit. Profit is one of my favorite words, and in my opinion, the most "American" word. Capitalism and profit are part of the foundation this country was built on. In general terms, capitalism to me is simply the belief that you should get paid for your hard work, risk taking, and creativity. The hard work is paying your dues, such as learning a business from the ground up, building start-up money, or finding people to invest in your idea. Risk is taking a chance. Your idea may not work and you could lose your money. Creativity is where your imagination kicks in. This is where your ideas come in whether you are making a new widget, or simply doing things better, cheaper, and faster. These three things combined get you from nothing to profit. Quite simply, profit is taking one dollar and making two dollars, legally. There are so many ways in this great nation to make a profit. It is the reward for taking a risk by pursuing your idea, dream, and passion.

To go a little deeper, profit is when your income, the money you bring in the door, is greater than your expenses, the money going out the door. The saying, "It takes money to make money," does have some truth. Ned's Shed needed money to make money. MoneyBags needed money to rent a building that housed the BBQ-ice cream shop. He also needed money to buy ingredients and supplies to run the business. He needed money to pay the invisible expenses (utility bills: water, electricity, trash, and so on), to advertise, and to pay the people who worked for him. Therefore, when he purchased ingredients and supplies he would always try to sell them to other people for more than he paid. He needed to mark up his food enough so that he could pay all his expenses and still have money left over for himself: profit. Otherwise, why should he take the risk?

The reward for taking risk

If enough people did not buy food from him, he had three options to try to increase his profit. He could lower costs by changing to a cheaper supplier, avoiding expensive long-distance calls, or having fewer workers, among other things. Another option would be to offer specials, such as buying one and getting one for half price, in the hope that more sales would increase his profit. The third option would be to advertise to attract more people to buy his food. To leverage his efforts, he would often do a combination of the three.

Your MoneyBags Mission

A quick game your young kids can play that allows them to be their own boss is on the PSB Kids website (http://pbskids.org/itsmylife/games/boss/). This site shows them the steps an owner needs to think through, and they can choose different options on how to handle their business problems. Also, make sure to read the book *What Color is Your Piggy Bank? Entrepreneurial Ideas for Self-Starting Kids* by Adelia Cellini Linecker.

Another fun exercise is to illustrate all of the steps required before a business owner realizes a profit. Go through your house and pick out different items. Discuss what was involved to bring it from nothing to your house. For example, orange juice goes through a long process and several costs before making it to your dining room table.

$ First, the farmer has to buy or lease the land.

$ Then he has to buy or grow the orange trees. Go online to see how long it takes before an orange tree produces oranges. Is it one, two, or more years?

$ While he is growing his crops, he has to make sure they are watered and protected from pests.

$ Once the trees produce fruit, the farmer has to pick the oranges. If he has one hundred trees and each tree has fifty oranges, he needs to hire and pay staff to help him harvest the fruit.

$ Furthermore, the orange trees become rather tall—how do the pickers reach the oranges on the top? Do they use tall ladders or does the farmer need to create or purchase a special tool? Both options cost money.

$ Once the oranges are picked, how does the farmer transport them to the place to make the orange juice? Does he have a long conveyer belt or does he have to move them with trucks?

$ Now that he has the oranges in from the orchard, how does he make the juice? What ingredients does he need? Have your kids read the ingredients on your orange juice carton.

$ Where does he get the cartons and how much do they cost?

$ How does he fill some cartons with pulp-free juice and others with extra pulp?

$ What does he do with all the orange skins?

$ Okay, now that he has figured all that out, he needs buyers or stores that want to buy his orange juice. How does he find buyers? Does he need to advertise?

$ Once buyers are secured, he needs to get the cartons to the grocery store without the orange juice spoiling, so he has to have a fleet of trucks or pay truckers to haul the juice for him.

$ Once the juice is to the store, the farmer hopes enough customers choose his brand so that the grocery will buy his future harvests. So he needs to market to get your attention, which also costs money.

$ The farmer also needs an accounting system in place to track all the costs of running the orchard and track which stores have paid him for his product.

Do your kids realize that all of these steps cost money and that the farmer has not yet received a penny of profit? So, let's assume that it costs $27,000 to produce the harvest. If he produces 17,000 cartons of juice he needs to charge $1.59 per carton ($27,000 / 17,000 = $1.588). If the farmer wants to have a profit of $24,000 he needs to charge $3 ($27,000 cost + $24,000 profit = $51,000 gross income, $51,000 / 17,000 cartons = $3).

If you live in the country, visit a farmer to see what it takes to get the food on your table. If you live in the suburbs or city, go to a local small business and ask the owner what they do to make a buck.

For a week, instead of buying orange juice, consider having your kids make it, without a juicing machine. Simply purchase the oranges and have your kids cut and squeeze out the juice into a glass. How many oranges did it take to fill up a large glass? How much did it cost to make? If you were going to sell it, what price would you set if you wanted to make a 20% profit? Assume the oranges cost a dollar each and it took 4 oranges (4 x $1 = $4, $4 x .20 = $0.80, $0.80 + $4 = $4.80). How did it feel to squeeze the oranges? Did it taste a little sweeter since you did all the work? Did your kids' hands get a little sticky?

This summer, consider encouraging your kids to open a lemonade stand. Walk them through the different steps involved to make it profitable.

$ Have them take their allowance Spend money and go to the store with you to purchase the ingredients and supplies.

$ When you return from the store, look at how much they spent on ingredients and supplies. Let's say $10. Now they need to figure out how much to price the lemonade. First, they need to calculate their break-even point (income = expenses). For example, if they price a cup at a dollar they need to sell 10 cups ($10 / $1 = 10 cups), or they could price it at fifty cents, and

Profit

then they need to sell 20 cups ($10 / $0.50 = 20 cups).

$ Profit comes after they make their expense money back. So if they want to target a 25% profit and they decided to price the lemonade at fifty cents, they need to sell 25 cups ($10 x .25 = $2.50, $2.50 + $10 = $12.50, $12.50 / $0.50 = 25 cups) to make two dollars and fifty cents in profit. What if they wanted to make a 50% profit ($10 x .5 = $5, $5 + $10 = $15, $15 / $0.50 = 30 cups)?

$ What system will your kids put in place to keep track of their sales? Have them either write the names of their buyers down on a piece of paper (future client list) or simply draw fence posts (for each cup sold, draw a line, up to four, then on the fifth sale draw a line across). Another option is to count the number of cups that they start with and then subtract the number of cups that they had when they closed. The difference is the number that they sold. If they give a cup away or if one breaks, they need to keep track of it when using this method.

$ Where are they going to place this lemonade stand? Should they put the stand at the end of a dead-end street or near an intersection? If your house isn't the ideal spot, they can consider asking a neighbor if they can set up shop on his or her property. They may need to kick in a little money to "lease" the space, which will increase their cost, but would hopefully increase their sales to offset the cost. For example, if your neighbor said that they could pay in trade by giving them a glass of lemonade for a day of rent and your kids are trying to make a 25% profit selling it at fifty cents, now they need to sell 26 cups (one extra cup) to offset the added cost of using their neighbor's property for their lemonade stand.

$ What time of day may be best to sell? If you live in a large neighborhood and know most people return home from work between 5:00 and 7:00 p.m., that sounds like a good time. Your kids will also learn that the people they know will be more likely to buy from them than people they don't know. Hence, the importance of networking and good social skills.

$ How about advertising? If they make a sign with big letters versus small letters to tell people, the cost of a cup may improve their sales. Another option is to mimic MoneyBags and create a sandwich board sign to have your kids wear.

$ Since they will be dealing with cash, your kids will need to have a cash box to break larger bills. Consider thirty dollars broken down as eight singles, four five-dollar bills, four quarters, five dimes, and ten nickels. If you lend your kids money, remember it needs to be paid back to you.

$ At the end of the day, determine how much money was made. How many cups were sold? Does the cash drawer balance? For example, if they sold 26 cups at fifty cents they should have thirteen dollars (26 x $0.50 = $13) plus the amount that started in the cash box ($13 + $30 = $43). If they are short, what happened to the money? It could be as simple as forgetting that one of the cups got damaged, or maybe they did not count money back properly. If they are over, it is likely that they forgot to write someone's name down or make a fence post.

$ Have your kids calculate their profit or loss ($13 sales - $10 cost = $3 profit). Did they hit their 25% profit goal? Did they exceed or fall short of their goal? If they do it over multiple days or weekends, they should track their sales to see if there are any trends. Assuming it was a profitable day, have your kids return the $10 to their Spend jar and then have them divide and allocate their profit money up into the four pots (MoneyBags Savings, 25%; taxes, 25%; charity, 10%; and spend, 40%).

Chapter 44
Marketing is a Double-Edged Sword

To make money, you need to provide a good or service that someone wants. To be good at this, you have to reach many people to let them know what you have and why they want it; thus marketing was born. Marketing is a way to help build awareness that a product or service exists. However, just because it exists does not mean you should spend your money on it.

Marketing is so intriguing. As a business, if you do it right, you can hit it out of the ballpark and make lots of money. Nevertheless, because there is so much competition for your buying dollar, it is hard to stand out. Seth Godin wrote a fabulous book, *Purple Cow*, which explains the importance of being different. MoneyBags owned Ned's Shed from approximately 1952–1972. Since that time, things have changed. In his day he was cutting-edge in mimicking Burma-Shave signs, displaying simple billboards, and placing random calls down party lines. Today we see billboards every-where—roads, bathrooms, gas pumps, and so on. We get advertisements emailed or pushed onto our smart phones, not to mention every web page is selling some-thing. The movie *Minority Report* gives us a glimpse of how creative advertisers may be in the future by sim-ply scanning our retinas as we walk through the mall. Companies are constantly trying to figure out how to fulfill our changing wants, get our attention, stay top of mind, and create brand loyalty.

It is your job to be aware of all the marketing bom-barding your kids on a daily basis, from breakfast cereal to cartoons to candy to clothing.

Your MoneyBags Mission

The next time you go shopping, look for the promo-tional, gift-with-purchase marketing. Do they offer a necklace with a book? Ask your kids what they really like, the book or the necklace? How about fast food meals, cereal, or candy with toys?

Over the next week, when you are watching TV with your kids, make a concerted effort to focus on what is being sold. Asking your kids if they NEED it or WANT it (Chapter 5). Going forward, when you see an ad or your kids go nuts for a certain item, remind them that there will always be new and shiny things.

For fun, visit the PBS Kids website and explore what they say about spending and money smarts.[5]

Every time you see a commercial or billboard, simply ask your kids, "What are they selling?" I realize that sometimes you may want what they are selling, to organize, simplify, or enhance your life, but often it is an impulse. Many people buy things because of a perceived "cool" factor, but they do not need and will hardly use the purchase.

Make it a game with your kids. When you go to the store and they point out a targeted ad, say, "BUSTED . . . I know you just want my money . . . BUT I AM SAVING IT, CHA CHING!" as they do a silly money dance!

---

5.   PBS Kids website for money smarts: http://pbskids.org/itsmylife/money/spendingsmarts/index.html (Accessed July 2011).

Chapter 45
The Impact of Stealing

If you have not done so already, explain to your children why stealing and shoplifting are wrong. As you know, there are many reasons that stealing is wrong, but one of them is financial.

When I think of stealing, the original cartoon *How the Grinch Stole Christmas* always pops into my mind. I remember him slithering around the house, taking everything in sight, including the candy canes in the sleeping children's hands. Stealing from people, like the Grinch did from the Whos, means taking things that cost someone money. On a basic level, the person whose possession is stolen has experienced a loss or financial setback by the dollar amount of the items taken.

Often, people rationalize that theft from a business is no big deal because it is an entity and not a person. Well, MoneyBags was a person, my father is a person, and many other businesses belong to people. However, let's look at a big company versus the mom-and-pop stores that my family owned. McDonald's is a large chain restaurant, but most of the restaurants are franchised, which means they are usually owned by someone locally. Other stores like Target are not franchises, but anyone can buy shares of their stock to become a partial owner. In cases like this, many people own the store.

If people take merchandise without paying, the business's profit will decrease. This is true for ALL businesses and the impact of it is huge. When someone shoplifts, it eliminates the opportunity for the stolen item to be sold. As a result, the business cannot sell it to recoup expenses already paid. The larger the loss from theft, which is called shrinkage, the more businesses need to compensate for the lower amount of money coming through the doors. A business is forced to either raise prices or reduce costs to offset the loss from shrinkage, which can mean laying off employees.

One thing to keep in mind with stealing is that it usually starts out small and progresses to a larger scale. As with the Grinch, stealing the candy cane was just as much stealing as taking all the presents and the tree.

Your MoneyBags Mission

Talk to your kids about how shoplifting is illegal. Explain the chain of events that occurs when someone is arrested for stealing. Go on the Internet and look up the legal consequences for shoplifting in your state.

When you go into a store dressing room, look for signs of shoplifting. In a clothing store, classic signs are empty hangers, price tags, or security tags on the floor. Is there a person monitoring the dressing rooms by asking you how many items you have and then giving you a number? Are the dressing rooms locked? Do you see merchandise locked up? Do you see strange uprights when you walk through the store doors, which are designed to trigger alarms if someone leaves the store without paying? The only reason stores take these precautions is to deter shoplifting. All these precautions cost money, reduce profits, and increase the price you pay for stuff.

Ask your kids if they have friends who download music for free. Do they realize this is a form of stealing? If they like the artist and want them to continue to write more music, why are they reducing the artist's profit? Have you ever seen people take newspapers or sneak into a movie? Is this stealing? Does it really matter?

Avoid other forms of dishonesty, such as buying an outfit for a special occasion, wearing it once, and then returning it. I am amazed at how many people think this is acceptable behavior. The value of the dress goes down greatly once someone wears it, just like a car that is driven off a lot.

Consider opening up to your kids by sharing your personal experience if you stole something as a child.

Explain what happened to you and what you learned from the experience.

If your child takes from a store because they don't understand the system of paying for an item, you have a few ways to react. Make it a MoneyBags Moment. Walk them back to the store, take them up to the counter, and simply explain the error to the clerk. Have your child return the item and apologize. Another option is to have your child pay for the item with their allowance money. This does not have to be a humiliating experience. It happens to little kids, but they need to know that their behavior is not right. Simply teach them the ropes.

The Evolution of Money

Chapter 46
Bartering

Why does money have value? It's just paper, right? Quite simply, it has value because people BELIEVE it has value. If lots of people stopped believing in the value of money, which we got really close to in the last few months of 2008, then the value of money would drop or disappear.

In the worst-case scenario, the value of the dollar becomes worthless. If that ever happens, something else like water, oil, food, or gold would take paper money's place. Basically, we would go to an old-fashioned bartering system where people traded things of value for other things of value.

Jack and the Beanstalk is a classic example of bartering. In the story, Jack is told to go to the market and sell the cow, but instead he ends up trading the cow for five beans that grow into the famous beanstalk. More recently, the movie *The Little Mermaid* shows Ariel bartering with Ursula the sea witch for legs in exchange for her voice.

Your MoneyBags Mission

For fun, have your kids look around your house to locate an item they think is valuable, such as a candy bar or pack of gum. Then have your kids practice bartering to trade it for something they want from someone else in the family, such as a small toy, computer time, or full control of the TV remote for an hour. Sometimes they may need to add in one or two more things to complete the trade. They can also barter with a service. For example, they might offer to take out the garbage or wash the dog in exchange for receiving their favorite meal or being allowed to pick their favorite restaurant for dinner.

Teaching your kids to negotiate is an important step. For the next week, focus on negotiation so your child can become more aware of ways to increase their own financial situation through negotiation.

Recently, there have been stories in the news of people bartering. One such story is about Kyle MacDonald, who started bartering with one red paper clip and traded up to a house![6] Check out Kyle's website, to read his story. As a family, consider doing what Kyle did and go to an online bartering website to trade up and up and up for something you want.

The game Monopoly (Chapter 14) is an excellent tool to teach bartering. The goal of the game is to get all the properties of one color. Sometimes other players purchase properties that you want or you strategically purchase a property to block someone's Monopoly. One part of the game is negotiating for properties you want that other players own. For example, if one player has two yellow properties (Marvin Gardens and Ventnor Avenue) and one red property (Kentucky), they may want to negotiate with another player who has the last yellow property (Atlantic) and holds the other two red properties (Indiana and Illinois). If you have not played Monopoly in a while, consider pulling it out, dusting it off, and playing it on game night.

---

6. http://oneredpaperclip.blogspot.com/

Chapter 47
Where Does Money Come From?

When I was a little and asked my dad for money, he would always say, "We don't have a money tree in the backyard." I remember thinking how cool it would be to have a money tree and envisioned it as the largest tree in our backyard with a million hundred-dollar-bill leaves!

If money does not grow on trees, where does it come from? Only governments are allowed to make money. In 1792, the U.S. government passed a money law, which is "an Act establishing a Mint, and regulating the coins of the United States."[7] As a result, the government created a standard currency, which makes buying and selling goods easier. For example, if everyone made their own money, then it would be like handing pieces

---

7.   http://www.constitution.org/uslaw/coinage1792.txt

of paper or other objects to people. My money might look like Monopoly money on colored paper, whereas someone else's money might be pebbles. If the money is not the same, how would you know which is more valuable? How would you determine who gives change to whom?

Due to the importance of one standard currency, it is illegal to manufacture money. This is called counterfeiting. When people make fake money, it hurts the value of the real currency. As a result, the government makes currency difficult to duplicate by using things like color-shifting ink, watermarks, security thread, ultraviolet glow, microprinting, and fine-line printing patterns.

Your MoneyBags Mission

Locate a $1, $5, $10, and $20 bill. Look at each one very closely to see all the unique things the government does to prevent counterfeiting. Do you see the serial number? Whose two signatures are on the bills? What titles do they have? Go a step further and look at it under a magnifying glass; do you see the red and blue threads? Pretty cool! Go online to ustreas.gov or www.secretservice.gov/know_your_money.shtml to discover the tricks the government employs to make it difficult to copy money. Consider taking a tour of a local bank, Federal Mint, or Federal Reserve Bank.

An excellent book to read with your kids is *Money Sense for Kids* by Hollis Page Harman, PFP. Though money has changed over the years, this book goes into excellent detail about the U.S. currency. With pictures of all the bills, it explains the significance of the person's portrait on the front, the importance of the pictures on the back of the bill, seals, serial numbers, and so on.

Finally, debunk the belief that you cannot have a money tree! Make this a MoneyBags Moment. As a fun celebration of money and the important role it plays in our daily lives, create a "Money Tree." Consider erecting the tree every year between April 2 (the enactment of the 1792 Money Law) and April 15 (tax day). Be creative with your decorations!

Chapter 48
What Happened to the Gold?

Years ago, gold coins were the traditional form of money. Robin Hood robbed the king of all his gold to give to the poor. Well, gold coins are really heavy to carry around and rather loud. As you can imagine, Robin Hood could hear the king coming from miles away, so it made him an easy target to rob.

When you have gold coins, where do you put them? When you become rich and outgrow your MoneyBag, you will need vaults to store it. One excellent example of the difficulty in handling large amounts of gold and coins is in the movie *The Count of Monte Cristo*. In one scene, the count wants to buy a large estate, and he pulls up in a wagon filled with gold coins and other treasures. As a result of this inconvenience and the risk of carrying such large amounts of money, banks, paper bills, and plastic cards were invented.

Moving physical money in large amounts is still challenging. When I was in college, I had the wonderful opportunity to work at Walt Disney World. The experience was the dream of a lifetime for a typical "Type A" personality who LOVES business. I got to see the inner workings of one of the best-run businesses in the world. However, being from a small town, I was a little overwhelmed. To this day I will never forget seeing my first armored truck. I was walking from the employee lot into the back tunnel entrance. The entrance was large enough to drive a truck through. There were always rumors that Disney made so much money so fast that they did not have enough time to count it, so they merely weighed it. I laughed and figured that this was a rumor until one day I stopped dead in my tracks watching the armored truck pull into the building for the money pick-up with four armed guards, one on each wheel, rifles out and ready.

Your MoneyBags Mission

Find one hundred pennies ($1) and a dollar bill. Give them to your kids to carry around for the day. At the end of the day, go into a store and buy a small item with the two dollars. Afterwards, talk about how it feels to be free of the heavy weight of the coins and discuss the reaction of the cashier when he or she saw all the pennies.

What Happened to the Gold?

To learn about interesting facts and the history of money with your kids, consider checking out the *Ultimate Kids' Money Book* by Neale S. Godfrey. This book covers a lot of ground at a high level, like money history, budgeting, banks, the economy, government, and investing.

Chapter 49
Why Do People Use Banks?

If you ever go to Siena, Italy, make sure you visit the world's oldest bank, Monte Dei Paschi Di Siena, which was established in 1472 "for the purpose of granting loans to 'poor or miserable or needy persons' at a minimal interest rate."[8] Can you imagine the changes the bank has seen over the years?

So why do people use banks? Banks have evolved over time as a way for people to protect, grow, and borrow money. Banks are safe, since they have vaults to store the money, versus a purse, wallet, drawer, mattress, or coffee can. If you have lots of money, it is hard to carry around and protect. Banks allow people to deposit their money, and the bank will hold it. Banks also pay people money to hold their money or charge money when they lend (see Chapter 51).

---

8.   http://english.mps.it/La+Banca/Storia/IlPrimoMontePio.htm

Note: *Credit unions are similar to banks, with two main differences. First, not just anyone can open an account at a credit union—you must be a member. Membership requirements are usually tied to one's employment, such as being a teacher or teacher's family member, but sometimes membership is regional for people who live in the same county or state. Second, credit unions are not-for-profit, which tends to lower costs to their members compared to banks, which are for profit.*

Your MoneyBags Mission

Introduce your kids to banking by exploring the Monte Dei Paschi Di Siena bank via their website (http://english.mps.it/). Take time to read about the bank's history and take the virtual tour of the old financial institution.

Next, take your children to your bank and explain to them the reasons that you chose this bank. People choose their banks for several reasons, including a location close to home or work, online features, friendly employees, good customer service, free checking, low fees, or good interest rates.

Take this time to re-evaluate your bank. Do the reasons you originally began banking with them still make sense? Do you even like your bank? If it is time to shop around, have your children go with you to a couple of different banks. One way to help evaluate banks is by asking for their fee schedule. The schedule lists the costs of services, including return check fees, wire fees, and monthly fees if your account balance drops below a set minimum balance.

I found an interesting statistic in reading Sarah Lorge Butler's article, "One Small, Surprising Way to Ensure Your Kid Gets to College." [9] She quotes from the College Savings Initiative, "Kids with a savings account in their own name are six times more likely to attend college than those without an account." How is that for incentive to teach your kids to save money? So go the extra step and get your kids directly involved. Because they have saved lots of money and you want them to go to college, take the next step and open a savings account in their name. Use the money set aside in their MoneyBag Savings.

---

9. http://finance.yahoo.com/news/one-small-surprising-way-ensure-070000810.html

Chapter 50
Safety Deposit Box/Vault

Like many people, I love the imagination of the *Harry Potter and the Sorcerer's Stone* movie. One part that sticks out in my mind is when Harry finds out that his deceased parents' had left him money, which was held at Gringotts, the wizard bank. This bank is not like other banks. It has all the traditional protections in place, but it is also run by goblins and protected by magic. The goblins escort Harry and Hagrid via a rail cart, deep underground below the bank. When they arrive, their escort goblin hops out of the cart to open Harry's vault. As with all safety deposit boxes, a key is required. Using Harry's key, they open the vault. Then you see Harry in awe as he looks at this room filled with gold!

Like Harry, we all would like to have a vault filled with gold. Many people use safety deposit boxes to hold their valuables, but it is usually in the form of important papers or jewelry. In order to have a safety deposit box, you rent a space from the bank. Since we don't have magic to ensure security, the box requires two keys to open—one you keep as the owner, and one that is held by the bank. When you want access your valuables, you tell the teller that you want to open your safety deposit box. They then require you to sign a card, creating a history of the dates and times you have opened the box, in the event a question arises. Just like the viewers did not know what was behind the door, the tellers have no idea what you keep in the box. Once it is opened, they leave you in private to review your contents, whether it's family pictures or gold bars. Since the bank does not know the contents in safety deposit boxes, it does not pay interest (Chapter 51).

Your MoneyBags Mission

Watch the movie *Harry Potter and the Sorcerer's Stone* with special attention to the vault scene. After the scene, pause the movie and ask your kids whether they felt the vault was safe and secure. Do they think the contents would have been protected if there was a fire? What do they think were items held in the other vaults by other owners?

If you have a safety deposit box or you need to open one, take your kids with you to experience the process you go through to access the box. If your bank will allow, let them walk into the vault and turn the key with the bank worker. If you are comfortable with it, let them look at the contents you have stored. Before you open the box, see if they can guess what is inside. For fun, have them place something of value in the box for safekeeping, such as a stuffed animal, pet rock, or two-dollar bill.

Chapter 51
How Do Banks Make Money?

In working with my clients I have learned that some of them don't understood how banks make money. To win at the money game, you need to know how it works. So how do banks make a profit?

On a high level, apart from renting safety deposit boxes, banks have two main functions: holding deposits and making loans. People often think that their money is just sitting in the bank's vault safely tucked away, like in Harry Potter. The reality is that if you want the bank to pay you money (interest), they have to put the money to work. This is the other side of their business: lending. People come to the bank to borrow money for large purchases such as a new car or house. For the bank to risk your deposited money for someone else to borrow, they create a formal and binding agreement called a loan. In that agreement, the borrower promises to repay the bank the money borrowed plus interest as a "thank you" for the favor. In turn, the bank gives its depositors a "thank you" for letting them use the money.

Here is how the process works. Let's say MoneyBags makes $10,000 from selling some ice cream machines. He doesn't need the money now, so he puts it into the bank for safekeeping and to make a little money. The bank takes his money and agrees to pay him 2% interest as a "thank you" for choosing them. A week later, farmer Bob needs to purchase a new pick-up truck for his farm and he needs to borrow $10,000. The bank checks out Bob's ability to pay back the borrowed money, via a credit report and basic financial information (tax returns, net worth, and so on). Once they decide that he has the means to pay them back and is a good risk, they give him $10,000 for the pick-up truck purchase. Bob promises to pay them back slowly, via a monthly payment, over five years at a 6% interest rate.

As a result of playing money matchmaker, the bank is netting 4% (6% received - 2% paid out = 4%), which is the spread. The bank's spread on the $10,000 is $400 a year (Bob $10,000 x 6%= $600, paid to MoneyBags $10,000 x 2% = $200, $600 - $200 = $400). From the spread, the bank must then deduct all of its expenses (rent, employee wages, and so on) to determine its profit.

To keep things easy, simple interest was assumed above. However, most banks pay compounded interest. For example, to calculate compound interest, in the first month MoneyBags will receive $16.67 interest on his $10,000 ($10,000 x (.02 / 12 months) = $16.67, $10,000 + $16.67 = $10,016.67). His new account balance is $10,016.67. In the second month, MoneyBags will receive $16.69 interest on the new balance ($10,016.67 x (.02 / 12 months = $16.69), amounting to $.02 more interest than he received in the first month. So his new account balance is $10,033.36 ($10,016.76 + $16.69 = $10,033.36).

Your MoneyBags Mission

As a family, go to your bank in person or online and look up the interest rates they are paying on savings accounts and charging for auto loans. Calculate the bank's annual spread using simple interest for $25,000.

To teach your kids about loans, go through the process of asking your kids if you can borrow money from them, and then write them an IOU. Pick a date for when you will pay them back and the amount of interest you will pay them for that favor. For example, ask to borrow five dollars for one week and you will pay them a nickel in interest. So after one week they will have gone from $5 to $5.05. Explain that they can lend out money and that THEY set the terms. Hence, they can request the money back in a week or a day and draw up the agreement accordingly. However, if the borrower does not accept the terms of the lender then no money will be lent.

Furthermore, you need to explain to your kids that some people may not pay them back despite their promise. This could be due to tough times or outright defiance. They need to be careful when choosing who to lend money to, just like the bank. It is important to always have a signed agreement (go to MoneyBagsLife .com for a free agreement) with the terms in writing so no one forgets the details of the agreement (family members included).

As a family, re-watch *It's a Wonderful Life*, but this time, watch for the financial workings of the Bailey Building & Loan. What caused the run on the bank and Bailey Building & Loan? When people panicked and wanted to pull all of their money out, what happened to the bank? How did George stop the run on the Bailey Building & Loan? Why wasn't the money in the vault to pay them back? As a family, mimic the money dance George and the workers do after they manage to survive the run on the Bailey Building & Loan, "Momma Dollar and Papa Dollar."

For fun, consider making a batch of Amish Friendship bread with your kids to get them excited about interest. Explain to them that Amish Friendship bread is designed to be shared. It keeps giving like interest does when you have money at the bank. This bread is cinnamon sugared sweet bread that is a simple, but ten-day, process to produce. Once the bread is made, have your kids give a cup of starter and recipe to three of their friends so they can make the bread and pass it on to three more friends![10]

---

10. See the recipe at http://homesteepedhope.com/2006/10/10/ amish-friendship-breadall-you-need-to-know/ (accessed October 2013).

Chapter 52
Plastic Cards!

Oh, how I love plastic cards; let me count the ways! One, a plastic card is sleek; it can easily fit into my pocket. Two, it is discreet; no one knows how much money I have in my checking account or my spending limit. Three, it gives me fraud protection. Four, it often has other monetary benefits, such as miles, cash rebates, concierge services, and more. Five, cards give status recognition. A silver is better than a nonmetallic color card; gold is better than silver; platinum is better than gold, and some people don't even realize that there are black cards, which are the holy grail for the status climbers. Six, with a credit card I can buy it NOW with money that I don't have! Okay, I got carried away. See how easy it is to do?

If I were a child today, the first thing I would want is a plastic card with a magnetic strip. Think about it: when kids see the cards, they have no idea if they are debit or credit cards. How much money is on it: $1 or $1,000,000? All they know is it buys "stuff." It is important to walk your kids through the reasons why cards are so popular and the key differences between them.

Debit Card

A debit card is always connected to a checking or savings account. To obtain a card, you just need to open a checking account that provides a debit card; no underwriting is required. Like a check, when the card is used, it draws the balance down, so your "limit" is equal to your checking account balance. Debit cards usually have no annual fees, nor do you have to pay interest since you are not borrowing money. You can go to a store to make purchases or make a cash withdrawal at an automatic teller machine (ATM). Banks make money by charging a fee to the merchant when you use your card. To encourage use, some banks reward their debit card users by depositing a percentage of cash back into their account. Consider training your kids to call your debit card the Do-Right card, since you are using cash and living within your means. Note, it is possible to overdraft your account by withdrawing more than your available balance, which will result in a nonsufficient funds (NSF) fee.

Credit Card

A credit card looks just like a debit card, but explain to your kids that a checking account is not tied to this card. Instead, you need to apply for the credit card by completing an application. The bank reviews your financial history, credit score, and financial standing (income versus monthly debt obligations) before issuing the card. This card is a privilege, since they are allowing you to use money that you don't have on deposit. The bank is taking on risk, so they set a limit on how much you can charge, such as $5,000. Furthermore, credit card users can benefit from perks when they use their credit card, whether it is cash back, airline miles, hotel points, shopping, and so on.

Finally, when you receive the statement, you have a choice on how much you pay toward your debt. You can pay off the total balance, which is your best option, since no interest is charged. You can choose to pay the minimum payment, which results in an interest charge. Making only the minimum payment is the least desirable option, since it costs the most money long term due to interest charges. Lastly, you can pay any amount between the minimum payment and the entire balance.

A credit card comes in handy when people have unexpected emergencies, such as their car being towed or unexpectedly replacing their furnace. Consider training your kids to call your credit card the KAB-LUEY card.

Note: *Some people have a prepaid credit card, which is usually due to no or a poor credit history. In this case, the credit card company turns the credit card into a debit card by requiring a deposit, which becomes their spending limit. This type of credit card relationship allows the owner to build or repair their credit history.*

The Evolution of Plastic

The evolution to plastic happened for three basic reasons: convenience, safety, and cost reduction. Convenience was a big driver of the change. Physical money has disadvantages, such as bulk, and you always have to carry the exact amount, or more, for your purchases. Plus, if you lose it, it is gone, "finders keepers, losers weepers."

Plastic also keeps your money safe. With technology, debit and credit card companies can monitor your purchases to head off or prevent fraud. Several times over the last couple of years I have received calls from credit card companies asking me if I had made certain purchases. Things that trigger alerts are highly unlikely events such as a gas purchase in Minneapolis at 9:15 a.m. and a purchase for gas or clothing in Los Angeles an hour later. They also know my purchasing behavior. I usually use my card to pay for meals and gas

($10-$50), so they know it is odd to see three large retail purchases ($300–$950). If a card's number has been compromised, they simply freeze the account with a couple of keystrokes, which makes the card unusable and declined for future purchases. You are not required to pay for the fraudulent purchases and they will send you a new card with a different account number.

Plastic can also generate or reduce costs for banks and credit card companies. Debit cards lower the bank's check-clearing costs and reduce the amount of time that money is en route. Banks make money when you use your card by charging a fee to the merchant. To encourage use, some banks reward their debit card users by depositing cash back into their account. Credit card companies make money in many ways. They can charge an annual fee for the privilege of using their card. They also charge merchants if they want to allow this form of payment in their stores. Merchants don't enjoy the fee, but customers tend to spend more when charging compared to when they pay in cash. The most common way credit card companies make money is from the interest they charge card holders when they don't pay off their card balance every month.

Your MoneyBags Mission

Go into your purse and wallet and have your kids pull out all your plastic cards. Ask them to guess which ones are credit and which ones are debit. They might guess right or you have already told them which is which, but these cards look the same. If you are comfortable, ask them to guess your spending limits. If you are not sure, go ahead and look them up on their respective websites or statements.

For one of the credit cards, have your kids locate the interest rate that you will be charged if you don't pay off your monthly balance. Walk them through the cost of maintaining a balance of $10,000 for a year using simple interest. To keep it simple, assume no payments were made and the interest rate is 8% ($10,000 x 8% = $800). What if the interest rate is 16% ($10,000 x 16% = $1,600)? For debit cards, show them your checking account. Explain to them how the balance is your limit and it moves up and down as transactions clear your account.

Over the next month, have fun when you pull out your plastic. Ask your kids if they remember if it is a debit or credit card. If you are using your Do-Right card, let them swipe it and do a little debit dance. If it is a KABLUEY card, pretend to be startled, like the cash register shocked you, as you swipe it.

Make sure to give your kids the receipt and ask them to hold on to it since it is an important financial document. Then, in a couple of days, have your kids

Plastic Cards!

pull out the receipts. Go online to view your statement activity, and have them locate the transactions. Talk about what just transpired. Continue to teach them the full cycle; if you used a credit card, show them the bill when it arrives, and point out that transaction. Furthermore, have them watch you pay the bill. Do you go online and pay directly from your checking account or do you write a check? Either way will work, but make sure you let your kids see it clear your checking account or reduce/eliminate the balance on your credit card.

Conclusion

As I reflect on the writing of this book, the ultimate goal is to get you and your kids excited about saving money. I believe that excitement kicks in once you cross what I call Your MoneyBags Threshold. To me, this is that point in time when you suddenly see your money at work—versus you working for your money.

For some people, this occurred at a very young age when they learned about interest and dividends. For others, it is when they see their discipline of saving money over time actually accumulate into a large sum. No matter when the MoneyBags Threshold occurs, you have become excited about saving money and begin to think of ways to stop spending so you can save more.

In closing, I am a big believer in the Buddhist proverb, "When the student is ready, the teacher will appear." The information provided in this book is not new, but you were ready. Now that you have completed the book, please pay it forward by recommending the book to someone else who could benefit.

Furthermore, I would love to hear stories about your experiences when working through the book or questions you have that were not covered in the book. Please go to the MoneyBags website at MoneyBags Life.com to share your MoneyBags Moments, stories, or teaching methods.

Acknowledgments

This book did not happen overnight, nor did I do it by myself. So this section is dedicated to those who helped me make this book a reality.

To my immediate family: my parents, Phil and Louise; my sister Cyndi Thomas, nieces, Ashley Thomas and Paige Thomas; the memories of my grandparents, Ned (MoneyBags) and Imogene, and Herbert and Helen Green. My family has always been my rock and biggest supporters. Plus, many thanks to John Carter and his daughter McKenna for being a sounding board and helping me through the final edits.

Thanks to Carlos Rodriguz. I shared with him my idea early on and he saw the potential. He helped me see the big picture and pushed me through my deer-in-the-headlights reactions when I became overwhelmed with the details and feedback from early reads of the manuscript, so we could improve the end product. He spent many hours maintaining the energy, vision, and potential. He is a marketing guru and a wonderful friend. A special thanks also needs to go to Amber Appel, who helped Carlos and I work through the details. When we did not have time to do the leg work, she stepped in with great energy, focus, creativity, and her own unique view.

A special thank you to my little sister from the Big Brother/Big Sister program, Brianna Sykes-Miller, and her mother Yolanda Sykes, as well as Eric Saugen for his support and encouragement to develop the book when in was in its infant stages.

Thanks to Nancy Imholte, who is a good friend and the first person I shared the developed concept of this book with in March 2009. Her enthusiasm helped me see the long-term possibilities of this book and gave me the courage to proceed.

To my good friends Kris Petersen and Suzette Rothberg, CFP®, who gave me feedback, ideas, and allowed me to occasionally camp out at their houses for creative spaces as I wrote chunks of the book. As well as, my mentor John Schubert, CFP®.

Many people (ranging from authors, peers, business professionals, and managers) gave me their time to answer my questions on how to proceed and supported me in the process. Many thanks to: Doug Lennick; Ed Kelly, CFP®; Kirk Hulet; Gary Scwartz, CLU, ChFC, CRPC; Bill Williams; Cynthia Gerdes, Brett Storrar, CFP®, CFMC, Bruce Bates, Jeff Rose, CFP®; and Heidi Richert.

To the people who reviewed the book early on to provide valuable, honest feedback to get it to a better product today: Wendy Hirschey; Patty Tushie; Mary Pat Dennehy; Pat Comp; Sarah Berkbigler; Jeff

Acknowledgments

Wegge, CFP®, CRPC; Lloyd Woelfle, CFP®; Stacy Hebdon; Adam Hennings; Theresa "T" Aagesen; Maja and Joe Engeman; Erica Sick; and Heather and Steve Schierenbeck. A special thank you to Caribou Coffee! In the writing of this book I spent many hours in various locations. Their excellent coffee and mountain lodge environment allowed me to stay awake and tap my creativity. Lastly, to my clients: I have enjoyed working with you, getting to know you, and being a part of your life. I have enjoyed growing with you. I am excited when you reach your goals, I am scared when we have to hold hands during the tough times, and I am always grateful for our relationship and the trust you have given me. You have become a part of my family. Thank you!

About the Author

Wendy comes from a long line of entrepreneurs and was raised with small-town values. She found her respect for money at an early age from her parents providing early exposure via an allowance and working in the family business.

Wendy attended college at Eastern Illinois University, where she received her Bachelor of Science in Personnel Management and Master's in Business Administration. She entered the financial industry in an entry-level position at Minnesota's largest credit union and then joined a large financial planning company in 1994. She became a financial advisor in 1996 and obtained her Certified Financial Planner designation in 2002. She has been a Twin Cities FIVE STAR Wealth Manager award winner in 2008, 2010, 2011, 2012, 2013, and 2014.